DATE DUE		
FEB 8 '84		
OCT 29 '84		
APR 2 5 1989		
MAR 0 9 1990		
NOV 1 3 2006		

ALCOHOL PROBLEMS IN EMPLOYMENT

CROOM HELM BOOKS ON ALCOHOLISM PUBLISHED IN
ASSOCIATION WITH THE ALCOHOL EDUCATION
CENTRE

Alcoholism in Perspective
Edited by Marcus Grant and Paul Gwinner

Alcoholism Treatment in Transition
Edited by Griffith Edwards and Marcus Grant

In preparation:

Alcohol and the Family
Edited by Jim Orford and Judith Harwin

ALCOHOL PROBLEMS IN EMPLOYMENT

Edited by
BRIAN D. HORE AND MARTIN A. PLANT

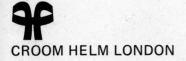

CROOM HELM LONDON

In association with the Alcohol Education Centre, London

British Library Cataloguing in Publication Data

Alcohol problems in employment.
  1. Alcoholism and employment
  I. Hore, Brian David   II. Plant, Martin
  658.38'2   HF5549.5.A4

  ISBN 0-7099-1202-1

Reproduced from copy supplied
printed and bound in Great Britain
by Billing and Sons Limited
Guildford, London, Oxford, Worcester

CONTENTS

PART ONE

THE GENERAL CONTEXT

INTRODUCTION

Brian D. Hore and Martin A. Plant

Since the Second World War rates of alcohol consumption have increased considerably in most industrialised countries. In association with this increase there has been a great proliferation of alcohol-related problems. These problems include clinically-diagnosed physical dependence on alcohol, as well as a much wider range of disabilities often attributable not necessarily to dependence on alcohol but to drunkenness. At a community level these problems have been reflected by increased demands upon treatment agencies, both statutory and voluntary. National Health Service alcoholism treatment units, private clinics, Alcoholics Anonymous groups and local councils on alcoholism have been established to meet the growing demand for help with drinking problems. Rates of crimes attributable to drunkenness have soared as have deaths from liver cirrhosis and other forms of alcohol-related mortality.

The traditional stereotype of the alcoholic was of an unemployed social derelict imbibing methylated spirits or other equally-unlikely beverages. In fact the overwhelming majority of problem drinkers do not conform to this image. They are mainly still in employment and some have extremely senior and important roles in commerce, the professions and industry.

Another myth besetting popular thinking about alcohol problems is that they are incurable. In fact, considerable reassuring evidence is available that many problem drinkers can be helped to overcome their difficulties and are able to resume normal lives. A further fact with particular relevance to employment is that industry-based approaches to dealing with alcohol problems often appear to be especially successful.

The misuse of alcohol contributes massively, if to an unknown extent, to absenteeism, inefficiency and accidents at work. The widespread nature and damaging degree of such alcohol abuse is now beyond dispute. This book is an attempt to review some of the evidence relating to the general effects of alcohol misuse on employment, the special problems evident in certain 'high-risk' industries and to describe some constructive approaches adopted in different countries to managing these problems.

1 ALCOHOL AND ALCOHOLISM: THEIR EFFECT ON WORK AND THE INDUSTRIAL RESPONSE

Brian D. Hore

It is frequently claimed that alcoholics or problem drinkers in industry cost industry in many parts of the world vast sums of money. In the United Kingdom for example a speculative figure of £40 million per annum is often quoted as the cost together with £20 million per annum in sickness benefit. (This figure is based on a population of 300,000 alcoholics earning mean national wages and losing an average of three weeks of work per year.) It has been suggested that alcohol problems may cost British industry as much as £350 million (National Council on Alcoholism, 1977). The awareness of the problems that alcoholism creates in industry has produced a different response in different countries. In the United States many large companies, e.g. Goodyear Rubber, US Steel and Du Pont, in recent years have developed industrial alcoholism programs (Von Wiegand, 1972) whilst in the United Kingdom such programs have been largely absent. A recent report on Health and Safety at Work does not mention alcohol as a cause of accidents (NCA, 1977). The purpose of this chapter is to examine three aspects of the problems of alcohol, alcoholism and work performance: first to look at the effect of alcohol on physiological variables connected with work performance; secondly, to examine some of the evidence relating to the effect of alcoholism on industry; and thirdly to examine critically industrial alcoholism rehabilitation programs.

The Effect of Alcohol on Physiological Variables

A variety of tests has been used for many years by investigators to assess the effect of alcohol on physiological functions. These include motor skills (such as a degree of body sway, finger co-ordination, reaction time, positional nystagmus and driving simulation) and sensory skills (such as corneal sensitivity, flicker fusion frequency, visual acuity, judgement of distance, pain threshold and olfactory acuity), together with psychometric tests, both verbal and non-verbal. It was shown as long ago as 1943 (Goldberg) that there was impairment of function on such physiological tests compared with controls at

10

surprisingly small blood alcohol levels, changes beginning when blood alcohol was on average in the range 0.31 to 0.65 per cent. It was noted that heavy drinkers were less influenced by the same dose of alcohol and this was not explained by differences in rates of absorption of alcohol from the gastro-intestinal tract nor from body distribution of alcohol or rates of disappearance from the blood-stream. It was clear that this difference was in fact due to a central brain effect and was an example of habituation. In other words the degree of intoxication and performance impairment in relation to alcohol, besides being related to blood alcohol level, is affected by a person's general drinking habits. Apart from habituation, such obvious factors as previous food ingestion (which will delay alcohol absorption) and type of beverage used, it was also shown that previous basal skill level was important, impairment being less likely on tasks where there was a high level of previous skill. There has not been agreement as to the effect of personality in relation to alcohol impairment and the matter remains undecided. It is important to note on many of these tests that as performance deteriorates under the influence of alcohol in a manner similar to that of the effect of oxygen deprivation, the person became increasingly confident. This was shown in assessing driving skills using tests which involved driving vehicles through increasingly narrow gaps (Cohen, Dearnley and Hansell, 1958). Skills such as driving are more affected by alcohol when coincidental tranquilliser medication is given (Matilla, 1976).

Problems Arising from Alcohol Abuse in Industry

There are two major measures of this, absenteeism and industrial accidents, both in general being increased in relation to alcohol abuse. There have been many studies of these problems some of which are quoted here. One of the early studies in the United States of America in a steel mill (Stevenson, 1942) found that three per cent of the male workforce missed time through drinking. The average worktime lost by each of the 352 workers was 22 days per year. The heavy drinking sample came from all the work groups and was correlated with middle age, an increase of indices of social pathology such as divorce, separation and a lower educational background. A study in the UK examined males attending an alcoholism treatment unit and found that half of the sample of 200 had lost time off work in their early thirties (Glatt and Hills, 1965). Further studies in the United Kingdom have come from clients attending community-based clinics, i.e. alcoholism information centres (Edwards *et al.*, 1967). It was found that 98 per cent of the workforce admitted they had lost time from work due to their drinking. The amount of work lost was staggering, 86 days per year on average. In relation to lateness for work 66 per cent of the sample were often late for work and 61 per cent reported being absent on Monday mornings (Edwards *et al.*, 1967). A recent study from Sweden confirms absenteeism and low productivity. This examined 868 patients attending 17 alcoholism clinics in western Sweden and recorded how many months they had worked outside hospital institutions during 1970. They were divided into three age groups: 20—49, 50—9 and 60—6 years. The 20—49 age group had worked on average for 50 per cent of the year whilst the older age group had worked for only 25 per cent of the year. A low productivity record was reported by 40 per cent of the patients in the 20—49 age group and by 70 per cent in the top age group (Berglin and Rosengren, 1974).

Although absenteeism is usually covered by medical certification it has long been suspected that certification will frequently not include the terms alcoholism or problem drinking. An important study in the UK examined sickness certificates obtained from the Department of Health and Social Security records of patients attending an alcoholism treatment unit in north-west England and found on average that in the previous year there had been 70 days' loss of work if the person was now in employment and 208 days' if the person was out of work at the time of initial examination at the clinic. The most interesting feature however was that of the reasons for absenteeism. According to the medical certification 36 per cent had been given a psychiatric diagnosis whilst ten per cent were considered as having accidents and 14 per cent respiratory disorders. It is important to note that *only* three per cent had alcoholism recorded on their certificates (Saad and Madden, 1976). A study in the United States on employees with drinking problems found that accidents, muscle and joint complaints (backache, arthritis, etc.) and digestive disorders were the principle reasons for certification (Pell and D'Alonzo, 1970). Whilst the above studies are important it is of further interest when the studies are controlled. An American study examining 10,000 subjects found that from medical records the alcohol abuse group had 2.5 times the absenteeism rate due to other factors of eight days or more compared with controls (Observer and Maxwell, 1959). A further American study found a rate approximately three times that of controls (Pell and D'Alonzo, 1970).

Industrial Accidents

The former American study in relation to industrial accidents found an accident rate of an alcohol abuse group to be three times that of the control group (Observer and Maxwell, 1959). In males accident rates were higher in younger men with alcohol abuse than with older men. It is possible that older men realise the danger and thus avoid being detected. Alternatively of course it may be that the older men are more skilled at their task and therefore impairment is less marked. A French study recorded blood alcohol levels of workers and found that the accident rate was as high in those with raised blood alcohol levels and also found that most accidents occurred in the afternoon (Gautier, 1965). Another study from France examined the involvement of alcohol in relation to industrial accidents. Twenty thousand workers in a variety of industries including heavy metal processing, textiles and mining were studied. It was concluded that seven per cent of accidents were caused by alcohol. When accidents which resulted in work stoppage were added, this rate became 15 per cent (Metz and Marcoux, 1960).

There are other ways in which alcohol can affect work performance. In an Australian study it was found that people who were heavy drinkers more often 'moonlighted' over jobs and were found to be more difficult for workmates to relate to and were generally more cantankerous and difficult as employees (Ferguson, 1973).

Management of the Problem Drinker at Work

Since the Second World War, particularly in the United States, there has been the development of industrial alcoholism programs, the purpose of which are to carry out early detection of the problem drinker and motivate that person towards treatment. There are two main reasons why industry should devise and carry out such programs.

First, firms can save money and avoid loss of manpower, reduce turnover of staff, impaired efficiency, training costs, accidents and absenteeism rates and enable sick pay saving to be carried out. A good example of the latter (Von Wiegand, 1972) is from the New York Transit Authority which has 34,000 employees and which has been running an alcoholism treatment program for many years. A study carried out in the 1960s over a five-year period in relation to sick pay showed that the saving on average was 1.5 million dollars *per annum* at a cost of 65,000 dollars *per annum* in running their program.

Secondly, it is said that industry effectively motivates the alcoholic or problem drinker towards successful treatment. It is frequently claimed that successful treatment of 50–70 per cent of the population is obtained in industrial rehabilitation programs compared with around 30 per cent from hospital treatment populations. This is not surprising in view of the motivational pressures of occupational programs and also the increased social stability of client groups with intervention occurring early before the client's social stability has been reduced, it being generally agreed that social stability increases the chances of success in alcoholism treatment. It should be noted that whilst this general trend of results of industrial programs would seem to be likely, it is very difficult in a scientific manner to prove the value of such programs. This however is of course true in alcoholism treatment services of all sorts and indeed treatment services for many non-alcoholic conditions.

Components of Alcoholism Programs

Much has been learnt from the United States, but it cannot always be inferred however that direct transfer of principles from there to other countries such as the United Kingdom is applicable. Development of programs in the United States began in the late 1940s, but the development was extremely slow and it is perhaps only in the last 15 years that major progress has been made. Occupational programs tend to have the following components.

To begin with it is advisable to have a *written company policy*. This states the procedure for identifying, confronting and referring employees who have a drink problem, irrespective of status, and specifies the distribution of authority and the responsibility for implementing such programs. Such information should be widely dispersed, especially as channels have to be established to enable the policy to be carried out. It is expected that such a policy will be based on negotiation jointly by unions and management.

Detection is usually based on *absenteeism and reduction of work performance*. Early industrial programs expected supervisory staff to diagnose an alcoholic or problem drinker. This is not satisfactory however as such supervisors are being expected to diagnose a condition which is frequently difficult enough for the professionals in the field and for which they are not trained. It seems generally agreed now that detection is best done in two stages. Initially it is based on absenteeism and decreased work performance. This in itself is a legitimate base for intervention as a reduction in performance and increased absenteeism represents a breach of employer-employee contract. Work supervisors therefore do not have to be alcoholism specialists, but what they do have to do is to detect changes in work performance and absenteeism. The second stage will be some sort of interviewing procedure carried out by other staff members who have been trained in alcoholism counselling. This will be to diagnose what is the cause of the absenteeism and reduced work performance. This approach, sometimes called 'broad brush', avoids alcoholism being seen as a special case. It becomes just one of the conditions that may account for absenteeism and decreased work performance.

Counsellors who are needed in the diagnosis and management of the alcoholism problem may come from a wide variety of backgrounds. In some cases they represent people who have been trained from inside the company. In other cases they are brought in from outside (Milstead-O'Keefe and Brooks-McLaine, 1979). An example of the successful training of lay people in this field has been shown in the United States Air Force in Europe. People without any social work or counselling background have been trained successfully in alcoholism counselling. The question may arise as to where within the company the counsellors lie. Generally they exist in departments such as personnel or medical; perhaps with the decrease in emphasis of the disease model of alcoholism there has been a shift towards this work being carried out more in relation to the personnel department. In different countries the type of external agencies used will depend on what is available. In the UK, programs have been frequently associated with regional councils on alcoholism although theoretically they could also be linked to AA and alcoholic treatment units. A problem however is that frequently external agents are already over-burdened with cases coming from a general population and cannot respond rapidly to industry's needs. Protection of job security and seniority are essential in any program, as clearly without such security the system will break down.

Problems of Industrial Programs

These have recently been examined (Schramm, 1977).

1. Attitudes of Unions. A recent review by an American union representative (Perlis, 1977) points out that in his experience there is resistance to the idea of 'job bugging' or medical snooping. Furthermore, workers do not always consider deteriorating job performances either to be the only or the most satisfactory method of detection.

Problem drinkers do not always perform badly and furthermore company programs should ideally offer help to all problem drinkers, not just those whose efficiency has decreased or who are frequently absent. It is considered that broad-based health and welfare programs urging employees to report all sorts of problems should be encouraged, that is a range of helping facilities should exist in which all those with problems can be detected and encouraged to come for help. In the United Kingdom union interest seems to have been very small, although recently union representation on a national committee in this field has been obtained (National Council on Alcoholism Report of the Working Party on Alcohol and Work, 1977).

2. *Management Attitudes*. It appears in the UK at least that there is resistance by management to the establishment of programs, both on the grounds that such policies may be seen as an index of managerial weakness and also that they may not be economically justifiable, and in the United Kingdom management interest, with a few exceptions, in this field has been largely lacking. Investigators into the problems of alcoholism and industry in this country have been hampered by attitudes of management personnel, who frequently deny any alcoholism problem in industry but do not allow investigations into their own companies.

3. *Management or Union Programs.* Although it has already been stated that occupational health programs in this field should be based on joint union management negotiations, this is not always the case. In some cases the programs are predominantly either union- or management-orientated.

4. *The Selection of Employees*. In industrial rehabilitation programs this is an important matter (Trice and Beyer, 1977). Unions frequently suspect that introduction of rehabilitation programs for alcoholism or problem drinking may result in more blue-collar workers than management being included in the programs. An American study (Trice and Beyer, 1977) bears this out. It was found that supervisors of relatively low-skilled employees were more familiar with and more likely to use a policy than supervisors of higher-skill employees. It is suggested that special training and special methods might have to be used to encourage supervisors to deal with high-status personnel and that training of such counsellors may have to create feelings of social distance between supervisors and their subordinates.

5. Evaluation of Programs. An important review of evaluation of occupational alcoholism programs has recently been carried out (Williams and Tramontana, 1977). Initially it is necessary to identify objectives, e.g. the objective may be rehabilitation of a percentage of staff with alcohol problems in a year, and such objectives must be related of course to the resources required.

Design for Evaluation of Programs

First, it must be decided what goals are to be measured (Williams and Tramontana, 1977). Frequently job performance and absenteeism are used, but these are not perfect criteria. Absenteeism, for example, is very variable and it is not always possible to be sure that an alcoholic employee is absent because of drinking behaviour. Secondly, an attempt has to be made to decide the methods for rating such changes. It is sensible to use as far as possible an objective approach rather than the subjective testimonial approach. Some authors have stressed the value of the raters being as independent as possible and coming from either other departments or indeed from outside the company, with the expectation that such methods will reduce bias. Again it has to be decided which changes are going to be measured in relation to the client group. It is clearly not possible to use the usual scientific method of a controlled trial in which one group receives treatment and the other group not, assignation to either group being random. A method frequently used is to treat each subject as his own control. It cannot be assumed however that the treatment is the only reason for any changes that are evident.

2 RISK FACTORS IN EMPLOYMENT

Martin A. Plant

Some occupations have well-established traditions of heavy drinking and in consequence suffer disproportionately from alcohol-related problems. The folklore about drunken doctors, lawyers, seamen, hoteliers, brewers and distillers is rich and well-known. In fact, there is considerable evidence supporting the conclusion that some jobs do have a 'high risk' of alcohol-related problems. In addition, there are several clearly-identified factors which help to explain why some occupations and not others do carry such risks. This evidence is largely derived from four sources. First, clinical studies have shown certain occupations to be over-represented amongst problem drinkers known to alcoholism treatment agencies. Secondly, studies of specific occupations have noted the extent within these of excessive or harmful drinking. Thirdly, alcohol-related liver cirrhosis mortality data clearly indicate that some occupations are vastly more 'at risk' in this respect than are others. Fourthly, some information is available from general population surveys.

Clinical Studies

The prevalence (extent in the population) of 'alcoholism' is unknown. The majority of those whose drinking causes problems do not come forward for help from treatment agencies. In addition, there is consierable disagreement upon the precise definition of what constitutes 'alcoholism'. Most alcoholism treatment agencies have been established only relatively recently. The self-help organisation Alcoholics Anonymous was founded in the United States in 1935 and probably did not become established in Britain until after the Second World War (Robinson, 1979). Not until the early 1950s was the first National Health Service specialised alcoholism treatment unit opened in England. The first such units in Scotland and Wales were not opened until the 1960s (Royal College of Psychiatrists, 1979). The local councils on alcoholism, under the auspices of the National Council of Alcoholism (in England and Wales) and the Scottish Council on Alcoholism were not established until the 1960s. Many were founded much more

18

recently.

Specialised agencies such as those referred to above certainly do not deal with all of the problem drinkers who seek help. General practitioners, social workers, the Samaritans and many other individuals and agencies are also frequently approached for counselling and advice. In addition, some problem drinkers contact not just one, but several, agencies for help with their drinking (Delahaye, 1977). Added to this is the fact that some agencies such as Alcoholics Anonymous do not keep formal records of who their contacts are. Clearly it is not possible to ascertain either precisely how many problem drinkers are known to agencies or what kinds of people these are. Inevitably one has to rely upon descriptions of individuals recorded by (usually medical) treatment agencies or by local councils on alcoholism. Such individuals may well be atypical even of those problem drinkers who are known to agencies. The latter vary greatly and may attract quite different people. Clinical studies provide a useful account of *some* problem drinkers in contact with *some* agencies. They do not form a basis for generalisation to problem drinkers not known to treatment agencies. The conclusions of some clinical studies will now be reviewed.

Clark (1949) reviewed the incomes and levels of occupational prestige of 1,695 white male alcoholics admitted to Chicago hospitals between 1922 and 1934. This study showed that such admissions were disproportionately men with lower-status jobs.

Lemere, Maxwell and O'Hollaren (1956) reviewed 7,828 private alcoholism patients in Washington 1935—55. Twenty per cent of these patients were businessmen or executives, five per cent were professionals and eight per cent were housewives. The 'average patient' was described as a 'male labourer, businessman or executive of approximately 40 years of age'. This review indicated that businessmen and executives were over-represented in relation to their numbers in the general local population. This could have been due to the limitation of the study to *private* hospitals which may attract a disproportionate percentage of affluent, high-occupational-status individuals. As noted by Spratley (1969) private facilities are relatively seldom surveyed. In consequence, groups such as company directors may escape attention for this reason.

Carney and Lawes (1967) compared 20 British male alcoholic patients with non-alcoholic patients and a control group from the general population. They did not discover any clear relationship between alcoholism and occupation. Even so, they concluded that the alcoholics were especially likely to have attained senior military rank.

Glatt (1967) noted that of 50 British private alcoholic patients whom he had treated during two years, 24 were company directors and ten were managers or senior executives.

Spratley (1969) sent self-administered questionnaires to 700 male members of Alcoholics Anonymous and private alcoholic patients in England. His results produced no clear evidence of an association between occupation and alcoholism. Spratley concluded: 'this preliminary investigation has indicated which occupations are potentially the most fruitful, namely the company director group. It has also been indicated that the regular services group is unlikely to be worth pursuing.'

Amark (1970), reviewing 199 Swedish hospitalised alcoholics, found that seamen, commercial travellers, those in artistic and literary professions, iron-plate workers, coppersmiths, butchers, dyers, drycleaners and shoemakers were over-represented. Commercial travellers were 13 times as frequent in this group of alcoholics as in the general population.

Mayer and Myerson (1970) described the biographical characteristics of 393 outpatients at a Boston alcoholism clinic. They concluded that there was no evident association between alcoholism and specific occupation.

Hore and Smith (1975) reviewed the biographical characteristics of 334 patients in 15 alcoholism treatment units in England and Wales. They concluded that while all occupational levels were represented, some occupations were excessively so. These were seamen, public house, hotel and restaurant workers, publicans, hoteliers, nurses, medical practitioners and company directors. Hore and Smith found that a higher proportion of the patients included in their review were from Social Class 1 than were the overall population of England and Wales.

In 1973 the Merseyside Council on Alcoholism reviewed the occupations of 2,000 alcoholics in the Liverpool area. Three-quarters of these were still in employment. While this review did not demonstrate an association between specific jobs and alcoholism, Social Classes 1, 2 and 3 were slightly over-represented.

In contrast, Wilkins (1974) concluded from a questionnaire survey of 546 patients attending a Manchester health centre, that alcoholics were significantly more likely than others to be of lower occupational status.

Three reviews have described groups of patients attending the Unit for Treatment of Alcoholism, Royal Edinburgh Hospital (Walton,

Ritson and Kennedy, 1966; Ritson and Hassall, 1970; Plant and Plant, 1979). All these studies concluded that individuals from Social Classes 1 and 2 were over-represented in relation to the general population of Edinburgh. Even so, the majority of patients in all three studies were manual workers. Plant and Plant (1979), in the third review, found that 64 of the 100 alcoholic patients they described reported having been in such 'high-risk' jobs as the Merchant Navy, the drink trade or the armed forces. An extremely high proportion, 34 of the 100 patients, reported having at some time worked as bar staff. No control group was used as comparison. Even so, it was possible, to compare the rate of 'high-risk' work experience of the patients with that of 150 Edinburgh male manual workers in 'low-risk' jobs, of whom only 35.3 per cent reported such 'high-risk' work experience (Plant, 1979a). This comparison strongly suggested that the alcoholic patients did have an unusually high level of 'high-risk' job experience.

Jindra and Forslund (1978), in a survey of 62 participating members of two AA groups in a western American city, found that individuals in two occupations were heavily represented. These were railway workers and those in the building and construction industry. Like many references of this type, no control group was used, nor was it stated how the representation of these occupations related to that in the general local community.

Studies of Specific Occupations

Much of the literature relating alcoholism and occupations is comprised of detailed studies of specific jobs. Such studies have provided considerable insight into the social processes that might generate excessive or problem drinking. Even so, most writings of this type are impressionistic and most have not used any reliable means of comparing the occupation they describe with other jobs.

Brewing and Distilling Workers

There is a well-known association between the drink trade and alcohol-related problems. Expressions such as 'drunk as a cooper' and 'drunk as a brewer' abound.

Three Austrian researchers collected self-reported alcohol consumption data and medical histories from 200 male brewers together with two comparison groups. These were 100 metal workers employed close to the brewery and 150 metal workers employed further away.

This investigation revealed that liver damage had occurred in 34 per cent of the brewers, a significantly higher rate than amongst the two control groups. In addition, the brewers reported that they were far heavier drinkers than did the control groups. Significantly, most of those who were suffering from liver damage were virtually free from side-effects and seemed fit to work. The researchers concluded that brewery workers need to be alerted to the dangers to their livers of excessive drinking. They also commented on the relationship between employment in a brewery with alcohol consumption:

> Experience has shown that this group of workers has an abnormally high beer consumption, due to the fact that each worker receives a substantial daily allowance of beer, plus the fact that consumption of beer at work is frequently uncontrolled. Heavy drinking for the brewery worker therefore carries no financial burden, consequently he has the opportunity to imbibe limitless quantities of beer. (Frank, Heil and Leadolter, 1967)

The relationship between brewing and distilling with drinking habits and alcohol-related problems has been further investigated in Scotland (Plant, 1979a). One hundred and fifty male new recruits to manual jobs in breweries and distilleries in Edinburgh were compared with 150 similar men newly recruited to 'low risk' jobs. These men were interviewed shortly after beginning their new jobs during 1975. One-third were sought for re-interview one year later and all were sought for re-interview between two and three years later.

The initial results of this study showed that brewing and distilling attracted a disproportionate number of men who were established heavy drinkers. In addition, recruits to the drink trade were significantly more likely than the control group to have poor work records. Once men entered either brewing or distilling, they were far more likely to report that they worked in an environment where heavy drinking was encouraged, even expected. This was so in spite of the fact that none of the companies included in this study allowed men to drink at work.

The follow-up results showed very clearly that working in brewing and distilling was associated with both much higher levels of alcohol consumption and, as time progressed, much higher levels of alcohol-related problems. As men moved from low- to high-risk jobs, or became unemployed, their drinking habits and levels of alcohol-related problems changed markedly. The evidence showed clearly that an individual's current job status was an important determinant of both drinking behaviour and related problems. Individuals who worked in the drink trade, Merchant Navy, or who became unemployed were very likely to drink more in consequence. Job changes were clearly related to changes in alcohol consumption. Several men left the drink trade in order to control their drinking in 'drier' work environments. Others became heavy drinkers or self-proclaimed alcoholics in 'high-risk' work environments where heavy drinking received strong social support. This study demonstrated quite clearly that those employed in brewing and distilling, often previously heavy drinkers, became even heavier drinkers and experienced far more alcohol-related problems than men in 'lower-risk' jobs. In addition, those in brewing and distilling had far more liberal definitions of what constituted 'heavy drinking' and were far more likely to report that they worked alongside alcoholics.

Coal Mining

Heavy drinking among coal miners has been widely referred to. Nyden has reviewed much of the literature in this field. He commented upon the fact that absenteeism and low efficiency in the coal mines have frequently been attributed to excessive drinking. A commonplace assertion is that the dangers of mining and the limited social outlets of some mining communities increase the pressures for miners to engage in heavy drinking: 'The ability to consume large quantities of alcohol, remaining relatively coherent and not missing work, is part of the self image many miners held.'

Beer gardens, bars and ethnic clubs play an important role in the social life of mining communities across Appalachia; pubs in mining areas in Canada, Great Britain and other mining countries play even greater roles, being involved with cultural, political and sports activities as well. Discussing drinking, one British miner commented:

> Another thing, of course, in the mining communities which you must respect is their capacity for beer — very important. Every Saturday night . . . on the wet beer of the counter, the face is propped up, the shots are fired, the coal's felled off and they get their belts bobbed up and all their new chocks in. (Nyden, 1978)

Nyden suggested four main factors which may account for the apparent (but largely unquantified) excessive drinking of many coal miners. First, miners have a strong 'occupational community' like other groups such as sailors. They exhibit a strong sense of solidarity, which combined with the paucity of social facilities in some mining areas, fosters heavy drinking in local bars. Secondly, the hazards of coal mining are exceptional. As Nyden remarks:

> The *Work in America* report takes note that alcoholism, drug abuse, and personality disorders stem partially from job insecurity, unpleasant working conditions or hazardous work; the report goes on to note that while little quantitative research has been done to detail these relationships, they have been extensively documented in clinical observations and records . . . The excessive use of alcohol by miners functions in part as a means to cope with stress related to constant hazards on the job. This stress also produces a high incidence of stomach disorders among miners; many report difficulty in eating while underground and the wide-spread use of antacid tablets, such as Rolaids. One young miner, when asked why he always ate the desserts in his lunch basket on the way to work, replied that he wanted to enjoy them while he knew he could, apprehensive about what might happen at work that day. (Nyden, 1978)

Nyden notes another occupational hazard that is characteristic of mining, ill health due to lung disease. The third factor Nyden identifies is the historical job insecurities of mining. Fourthly, he suggests that coal miners, in spite of increased automation in the pits, continue to have considerable autonomy at work. They are relatively free to socialise with their peers (which presumably reinforces the social pressures to drink).

Company Directors

Roman and Trice (1972) carried out a study of three American companies in which senior executives were alcoholics. The researchers concluded that if such senior individuals are incapacitated by drinking this may be taken advantage of by ambitious subordinates. In such a situation, problem drinking at work may be actively concealed or even fostered.

Domestic Servants

Straus and Winterbottom (1949) carried out an interesting study of drinking by female domestic servants in an American town. They interviewed 99 such women together with 117 females employing domestic servants. This study included 77 matched employer-employee pairs. The results showed that the female servants did have a higher level of alcohol consumption than the general population. Even so, there was no evidence of excessive drinking causing problems. The researchers speculated that any such women who did become problem drinkers would rapidly be dismissed from their employment. It was further concluded that the restricted social and sexual life of domestic servants encouraged heavy drinking.

Seamen

There is a well-known association between seafaring and a fondness for the bottle. This is discussed in detail in Chapter 5. An illuminating commentary on this association has been provided by a former sailor and abstinent alcoholic:

> Ashore part of the heritage of the sea are the visits to the houses of prostitution and the saloons and places where drink flows freely . . . new men are introduced to strong local drinks — cooliehow saki, calvados, or any other local wines, rums or whiskies. Then follows introductions to girls who would not receive a second glance from the same men sober . . . Their first objective is to outdo the old timers in regards both to women and liquor, until they have built up a tolerance and accustomed themselves to this life. (J.I.F., 1947)

J.I.F. further commented that the restricted life at sea encourages men to give vent to their repressed emotions on shore. Often this involves excessive or harmful drinking.

There is an extensive literature describing the drinking patterns and alcohol-related problems of both naval and civilian seamen. Powdermaker (1945) and Heath (1945) both concluded that roughly one-fifth of American merchant seamen passing through Merchant Marine rest centres were alcoholics. Wallinga (1956) described 94 hospitalised alcoholics who were in the United States Navy or Marines. He concluded that these men had developed drinking problems largely because of the social pressures to drink to which they were subjected while at work. Rose and Glatt (1961) drew similar conclusions from their study of 100 British merchant seamen. In addition, Rose and Glatt speculated that the Merchant Navy may attract men who are especially predisposed to become alcoholics. This view was shared by Brun-Gulbrandsen and Irgens-Jensen (1967) on the basis of a study of 3,447 young Norwegian naval conscripts. The researchers identified

14 per cent of these young men as alcohol abusers. Another Norwegian study by Arner (1973) examined the notoriously high accident rate amongst seamen. Arner concluded that at least one third of fatalities were associated with heavy drinking. Arner agreed with the speculation that seafaring may attract unusual men, in this case, those who are accident-prone.

Schukit and Gunderson (1974) reviewed the job types of 1,702 enlisted seamen in the United States Navy who were hospitalised alcoholics. The researchers concluded that the job preferences of naval alcoholics were broadly similar to those of civilian alcoholics. Jobs which had high alcoholism rates were of the administrative, clerical, deck and construction types, while technical jobs had low rates.

The prevalence of alcoholism in the United States Navy has been reviewed in detail by Kolb and Gunderson (1977). These researchers have noted that within the navy both men and women are expected to drink and are relatively encouraged to do so by the availability to all ranks of cheap alcoholic beverages: 'Estimates of prevalence in the naval population vary from 7 per cent "addicted" alcoholics (the same rate as in the civilian work force) to 38 per cent.' They report further that drinking problems are a major concern in the United States Navy, and that special treatment facilities, 'drydocks', have been established to cope with the situation. Reviews of naval alcoholics indicate that the 'higher-risk' jobs are mainly non-technical, while the 'low-risk' jobs are mainly skilled or technical.

Military Personnel

The high levels of excessive drinking in the armed forces have been widely discussed (e.g. Barrett, 1943; Harrington and Price, 1962; Maletsky and Klotter, 1975; Sclare, 1978b). Carney (1963), examining British service personnel in Cyprus, reported that military messes exert extremely strong pressures to drink. Gwinner (1976) has suggested that British military life provides a 'luxuriant medium' in which excessive drinking can develop and be perpetuated. The armed forces encourage individuals to conform, to be 'one of the boys'. At the same time military life produces boredom and frustrations. It is paternalistic and so the excessive drinker is supported and protected from reaching 'rock bottom'. In addition (like civilian seamen), service personnel frequently experience disruptions to their family life and males are frequently isolated from female company.

Long *et al.* (1977) have made similar observations in relation to life in the United States forces:

Since the military as a social organisation tends, by virtue of its paradoxical emphasis on masculinity and lack of autonomy simultaneously, to encourage the 'romance of alcohol' in which alcohol is seen to increase courage, sexual attractiveness and power, skilfulness and happiness, a powerful source of counterpropaganda is necessary to reduce alcohol abuse.

Oil Rig Workers

One industry which has many common features with seafaring discussed above, is the maritime oil extraction industry. Heavy or problematic drinking amongst oil rig workers has been widely alluded to, but there appears to be little hard evidence to justify this. Even so, oil rig workers are in an industry which, like more conventional seafaring, is dangerous, which isolates men for protracted periods and which provides them with exceptionally large amounts of money to spend while on shore leave (Kitchen, 1977).

Lawyers

Heavy drinking by the legal profession has been widely commented on anecdotally. James Boswell once recorded that he 'saw tonight what I never saw before: a company of advocates free from drunkenness' (Scott and Pottle, 1932, quoted in Rix, 1978). More recently a judge presided over court proceedings while conspicuously drunk. When questioned about this, barristers and court officials replied that they could do nothing since he was 'in charge'.

Doctors

The literature on alcoholism amongst the medical profession is nearly as extensive as that relating to the armed forces and is considered in greater detail in Chapter 4. Dependence upon alcohol and other drugs has long been noted as a major risk amongst doctors (Edwards, 1975; Ludlam, 1976; Noie, 1977; Talbott *et al.*, 1977). The most commonly-suggested reasons for the high alcoholism rate amongst doctors are that they are expected to be impervious to normal stresses and are a relatively affluent group (Ludlam, 1976; Murray, 1976a). Other explanations include long hours of demanding work and fatigue (Bressler, 1976) and the tradition of heavy drinking that supposedly exists amongst medical students (Duffy and Litin, 1964).

There is no doubt that studies of specific occupations which reputedly have high alcoholism rates have provided a great deal of useful information. Much of this is impressionistic and lacks the support of either control-group data or rigorous information relating to the general working population. Nevertheless, the literature reviewed above has suggested a number of plausible common themes, which are summarised later in this chapter.

Liver Cirrhosis Mortality

Excessive drinking can lead to liver cirrhosis. As the Royal College of Psychiatrists (1979) notes:

> This is an extremely serious and unpleasant condition, with a high expectation of death within a few years if the person then continues to drink. Both length of drinking history and level of drinking bear on the risk of liver damage — in effect, the concern has to be with 'lifetime' intake. There is some dispute as to what constitutes the safe level of alcohol intake, but solid evidence suggests that if someone drinks regularly the equivalent of between five and ten pints of beer or more each day, he increases this risk of contracting cirrhosis . . . Certainly when drinking is extreme and has averaged above ten pints of beer a day for fifteen years, the individual runs a grave risk of liver damage. Some research reports have suggested that as many as 80 per cent of drinkers in that sort of consumption bracket will damage their livers . . . Drinking is by no means the only possible cause of cirrhosis, but over recent years alcoholic cirrhosis has in this country gradually come to make a much larger contribution to the total cirrhosis death rate than was previously the case: in two studies conducted in Birmingham, the proportion of alcoholic cirrhosis rose from 33 per cent to 51 per cent of total cirrhosis cases, between 1959–64 and 1964–9. A recent study in South London showed alcoholic cirrhosis accounting for 65 per cent of the total cirrhotics.

Liver cirrhosis mortality is a useful, if imperfect, indicator of the prevalence of excessive drinking. Clearly this can only be taken as evidence of the numbers of excessive drinkers who have died, and not of those who are living (Kreitman, 1977).

The Registrar General's Office and the Office of Population Censuses and Surveys have produced liver cirrhosis mortality statistics which reveal that some occupational groups have especially high rates of death from this cause. The most recently published information is presented in Table 2.1 (Office of Population Censuses and Surveys, 1978).

Table 2.1: Liver Cirrhosis Mortality (England and Wales 1970–2)

Occupational group	Standardised mortality ratio
Publicans, innkeepers	1,576
Deck, engineering officers and pilots, ship	781
Barmen, barmaids	633
Deck and engine room ratings, barge and boatmen	628
Fishermen	595
Proprietors and managers, boarding houses and hotels	506
Finance, insurance brokers, financial agents	392
Restaurateurs	385
Lorry drivers' mates, van guards	377
Cooks	354
Shunters, pointsmen	323
Winders, reelers	319
Electrical engineers (so described)	319
Authors, journalists and related workers	314
Medical practitioners (qualified)	311
Garage proprietors	294
Signalmen and crossing keepers, railways	290
Maids, valets and related service workers	281
Tobacco preparers and product makers	269
Metallurgists	266

This table shows the 20 categories of occupation in England and Wales which had the highest rates of death due to liver cirrhosis 1970–2. Standardised Mortality Ratios were produced taking into account the age structure of each occupational group. The average occupation had a ratio of 100, so those included in Table 2.1 ranged from 2.7 to 15.8 times the average.

The 1970–2 data were accompanied by this comment:

Cirrhosis of the liver . . . has commonly been associated with high alcohol consumption and inadequate diet. Not surprisingly therefore, barmen, publicans and innkeepers as well as fishermen, deck and engineering officers and deck and engine room ratings, all units with high alcohol consumption, feature among the occupations with the highest mortality from this cause. For some of the occupations with high rates for cirrhosis of the liver, high alcohol consumption probably preceded the adoption of the occupation which was taken up because it afforded access to alcohol as well as providing the basic amenities of life such as board and lodging. For others, the occupation entails the separation of men from their homes, offering limited alternative opportunities for recreation.

That authors, journalists, medical practitioners and finance and insurance brokers should be among the occupations with the highest mortality from cirrhosis probably reflects quite different circumstances. Men in these professions often accept high alcohol consumption and inadequate diet as a natural consequence of the demands of their work. Alternatively, their social habits may reflect their reactions to the stress or pressures of this type of work.

Such links between occupation and alcohol are not new. More than 250 years ago Ramazzini remarked on the lethargy of men working in the distilleries of Modena and early decennial supplements commented on the drinking habits of workmen in certain trades. Farr commented that 'The majority of the publicans and the greater part certainly of wine merchants are temperate and as the mortality of the whole trade is high the mortality of the intemperate among them must be excessive.

The excessive alcohol-related mortality of those in the drink trade was also earlier noted by Wilson (1940):

Reviewing the figures of occupational mortality since 1860, it seems certain that the excess mortality among males (only) recorded as engaged in this trade has been not less than from 80,000 to 90,000 deaths. These figures do not include the excess mortality among other members (male and female) of the considerable army of persons engaged in this trade and liable to the temptations offered by alcohol.

General Population Studies

Some *general* information relevant to occupations is available from surveys of samples of the population. While these do not focus upon specific occupations, they do indicate important differences between manual and non-manual workers.

Self-reported data on drinking habits and alcohol-related problems are known to be inaccurate and usually under-reported (Plant, 1979b). Even so, the population surveys in Britain and elsewhere have confirmed that different social groups do have widely-differing drinking habits.

Four British studies have produced relevant results. All collected self-reported data from random population samples. Edwards, Chandler and Hensman (1972) concluded from their survey of a London suburb that, 'The general statement can . . . be made that more class I and II women are heavier drinkers and class I and II men are lighter drinkers than respondents in other classes.'

Dight (1976) concluded from her national survey of Scottish drinking habits that the heaviest drinking group in the population was young male manual workers. She also found that the proportion of regular drinkers was greater amongst high income groups for both sexes. In addition, she found that low income groups (mainly pensioners) had high alcohol consumption.

Cartwright *et al.* (1978) from their survey of the same London suburb originally investigated by Edwards, Chandler and Hensman (1972) concluded that: 'When consumption was controlled, occupational status groups I and II were the groups apparently most protected against experiencing alcohol-related problems.'

Plant and Pirie (1979) examined the self-reported alcohol consumption of population samples in four Scottish towns. This study indicated that non-manual workers of both sexes were more likely to drink alcohol at all than were manual workers. Even so, manual workers 'compensated' for their disproportionate abstinence rate by also being more likely than non-manual workers to be heavy drinkers.

Cahalan and Room (1974), reviewing two national surveys of American men, found that heavier drinking and alcohol-related problems were most commonplace amongst manual workers. Cahalan and Cisin (1966) concluded that amongst American men aged 21 to 39 those in high-status jobs were most likely to drink heavily.

General Conclusions

The evidence described in the preceding review clearly indicates that some occupations have especially high rates of excessive drinking. This conclusion is supported by clinical studies, studies of specific occupations, liver cirrhosis mortality data and in general terms by population surveys.

As noted above, a great deal of the 'evidence' linking alcohol-related problems and occupations is impressionistic, and lacks the support of control-group data. Even so, there is a considerable amount of agreement upon which the 'high-risk' jobs are and this is supported both by liver cirrhosis mortality rates and by the few controlled studies that have been undertaken (e.g. Frank, Heil and Leodolter, 1967; Murray, 1976a; Plant, 1979a).

As described above, there is a perplexing array of allegedly 'high-risk' occupations. What is there to link brewery workers with lawyers, or actors with seamen? Eight factors emerge from the literature as those most commonly suggested to explain why some occupations do have a 'high risk' of alcohol-related problems:

1. Availability of Alcohol. Some jobs provide workers with ready access to alcohol while at work. Clearly those in the drink trade and catering are particularly affected by availability. Other jobs make alcohol available by requiring its consumption as part of role performance. The salesman who is expected to wine and dine customers or the executive with a generous expense account are examples of this situation.

2. Social Pressure to Drink. Certain occupations have well-established and important traditions of heavy or excessive drinking. Coal miners, seamen, service personnel, medical students and those in the drink trade appear to be subject to such pressures.

3. Separation from Normal Social or Sexual Relationships. It has been suggested that excessive drinking is fostered if individuals are forced to work for long periods in a single sex setting or away from home. Commercial travellers, seamen, oil rig workers, service personnel and domestic servants have all been cited as examples of this factor.

4. Freedom from Supervision. If a worker is of high occupational status and not under close supervision it is easier to cover up impaired job performance or to drink heavily. Company directors, lawyers, doctors, and other professionals and commercial travellers or others with travelling jobs are workers without close supervision.

5. Very High or Low Income. Individuals with high incomes such as doctors and other professionals are clearly able to afford a high alcohol consumption. At the other extreme, those with low incomes may seek comfort in the bottle.

6. Collusion by Colleagues. An individual's drinking problems are often covered up by fellow workers for humanitarian reasons — to shield that individual from sanctions. Alternatively, a worker's impaired efficiency may be exploited by others seeking to gain influence or status at his expense.

7. Strains, Stresses and Hazards. Many of the 'high-risk' jobs have unique responsibilities, problems or risks. It has frequently been suggested that such pressures contribute to heavy drinking as a form of consolation or tension release. The dangers of coal mining, military service, seafaring or off-shore oil extraction, the job insecurity of the acting profession and the responsibilities of medicine or big business are examples of such stresses.

8. Pre-selection of 'High-risk' People. It is possible that some jobs, such as medicine, the Merchant Navy or the drink trade, recruit people from particular kinds of backgrounds or who are for some other reasons predisposed to become excessive drinkers.

Clearly, only some of these eight factors apply to certain occupations. In addition, there may be other reasons why some jobs either attract potential heavy drinkers or generate alcohol-related problems. The evidence clearly supports the conclusion that some occupations do have much higher rates of heavy drinking and alcohol-related problems than others. Consequently, an individual with whatever family background, religious beliefs or personality type, is far more likely to become a problem drinker in some work settings than in others.

PART TWO

OCCUPATIONAL STUDIES

INTRODUCTION

Martin A. Plant

As indicated by the reviews in Chapters 1 and 2, there is abundant evidence that alcohol misuse can, and often does, play a seriously harmful role in employment. In addition, it is apparent that the effects of alcohol misuse are especially prevalent, or at least conspicuous or a cause for concern, in certain industries.

Part Two presents a selection of recently-conducted empirical studies of drinking habits and alcohol-related problems in specific industries. In Chapter 3 Dr John Davies describes a study of five industries in the Glasgow area. In Chapter 4 Dr Robin Murray examines evidence related to the medical profession and in Chapter 5 Dr Keith Rix describes his study of alcohol problems amongst trawlermen in the north-east of Scotland. Chapter 6 is a more general chapter on alcohol and occupation, but with some special reference to the metal industry in the east of France. Chapter 7, an American contribution by Dr F. James Seaman, summarises a large-scale survey of United States railway workers. Each of these chapters provides a valuable contribution to the literature. In each, empirical data are presented which together illustrate some of the evidence supporting the view that alcohol problems in employment are both detectable and a major cause for concern.

3 DRINKING AND ALCOHOL-RELATED PROBLEMS IN FIVE INDUSTRIES

John B. Davies

This chapter gives an account of a study carried out on Clydeside, a heavy industrial region situated close to Glasgow, on the River Clyde. The material presented is a very-much condensed account of a larger study, *Alcohol and Work* (Davies, Cochrane and Marini, 1977–8) produced for the Scottish Council on Alcoholism in 1977–8. The account is selective and does not include all findings from the main study. In addition, there is more evaluation and speculation in the present chapter. The intention is not simply to report data and analyses, but to offer comment and interpretation in the hope of stimulating discussion of central issues. A more comprehensive account of the data and analyses is available in the main report. Finally, the views expressed in the discussion section are not all directly related to data obtained from the study, and range over a number of issues, some of which are of general rather than specific relevance. The views expressed are those of the author, and do not necessarily represent the views of other individuals or bodies concerned with this project.

In May 1977 funds were provided for a study of alcohol consumption by workers employed in industry on Clydeside. The reasons for increased interest in the use and abuse of alcohol by those in employment are well known, and only the briefest summary of these is given here. One important factor in stimulating concern has been the number of speculative estimates of the economic cost of alcohol(ism) to the nation as a whole; whatever the accuracy of these rather variable estimates, it appears that they all indicate a considerable sum. In addition, there are also important individual costs in economic and human terms which make such a study worthwhile. Until recently, there has been an almost total absence of data on drinking problems in industry in Scotland, a paucity which has been highlighted by Plant's (1979a) study of alcohol production workers and workers in other industries, and Rix's observations of a sample of alcoholic patients from the north-east fishing industry (see Chapter 5). By contrast, major normative studies of general populations have been carried out more

frequently. Dight (1976) has surveyed Scottish drinking habits
generally, and a similar type of study is currently being conducted by
de Roumanie (1979). Normative studies of development of drinking
and associated attitudes, from childhood to late adolescence, have
been carried out in Glasgow and central Scotland (Jahoda and Cramond,
1972; Davies and Stacey, 1972; Aitken, 1978). A number of other
studies may be cited. Whilst many of these studies show relationships
between alcohol consumption and social class none of them has
investigated how the employment class-structure in, and between,
different industries is related to the differential occurrence of heavy
drinking and/or alcoholism in those industries. Indeed, such investigation is explicitly beyond the realm of several of these studies.

At a more general level, *per capita* consumption of alcohol has
risen considerably since the mid-1950s; it appears that more young
people are starting to drink at an earlier age, and that the number of
young alcoholics in their twenties and thirties has increased sub-
stantially. The *Brewers Society Statistical Handbook* (1976) shows a
per capita increase between 1959 and 1974 of 47 per cent for beer,
124 per cent for spirits, and 284 per cent for wine. Dight (1976)
showed a reported reduction in the age at which young people start
their drinking careers, and Ritson (1968) and Glatt (1976) report
the increasing numbers, and poor prognosis, of young alcoholics
presenting for treatment. Finally, there is evidence which shows a
close relationship between *per capita* consumption and the incidence
of excessive drinking in a given population, which suggests that there
might be a causal connection between the rising *per capita* consumption
and the increasing reported incidence of alcohol-related problems
(Royal College of Psychiatrists, 1979).

The present study, therefore, is a response both to the specific lack
of data on alcohol problems in Scottish industry, and to the more
general awareness of an increasing alcohol problem, of which the
industrial problem is a part.

Method

Although in principle there are three broad ways in which people's
alcohol consumption may be studied, in practice only one of these is
feasible in the context of the present study.

It is possible to monitor the alcohol consumption of relatively small
groups of people by means of observational techniques. Such direct

observation methods have in fact been used in public bars in Edinburgh, and the methods used in this and other similar studies are described in Plant *et al.* (1977). These methods remained impractical for the present study due to the resources in manpower and time required to carry out such a study with adequate controls. In addition, there are ethical considerations in observing people's drinking behaviour with a view to relating this to work performance. It may be argued that an infringement of personal liberties takes place where observational data are used in this type of way.

Certain physical/physiological measures (e.g. blood-alcohol level, the 'breathalyser') can also be used. Little needs to be said about these, other than that their use to assess the alcohol consumption of workers engaged in tasks at their place of work would be highly un-wise, and unlikely to meet with any success at all. There would be justifiable resistance to such methods.

What remains are the much-used survey/interview techniques which tend to predominate in this area of research. There are clearly dis-advantages to using interviews and questionnaires, since the accuracy or truthfulness of verbal responses is always in some doubt, and there are usually no behavioural or physiological data against which to validate responses. On the other hand, these techniques are more acceptable to the majority of people and experience suggests that a 20-minute interview may even be a pleasant break from work for many individuals. In addition, where data confirm previously known facts, and where reliable and systematic differences regularly occur between the responses of different types of respondent, the researcher may have a high degree of confidence in the data and take serious account of instances where *new* facts come to light. The pre-cautions which can be taken, both during the construction and administration of interview/questionnaire schedules, and during the stages of data processing, have been outlined previously in Davies and Stacey (1972).

An individual interview technique was chosen, in which both verbal questions/answers and a number of short self-completion questionnaires were included. Interviews, which were anonymous, were conducted by two experienced female interviewers (both graduates who underwent a training period) and lasted for approximately 20 minutes each. The areas covered by the interview included: self-reports of consumption during the previous week, and the relationships between these reports and demographic variables; self-reports of lunch-time drinking; reported incidence of drunkenness and general effects of alcohol on work performance; and attitudes and opinions towards alcoholics and their treatment. In addition, firms which took part in the study were asked to provide data from their records of a general nature (i.e. *not* data which would enable individuals to be traced) about absenteeism, reported accidents, and any reported alcohol-related incidents. Short self-completion questionnaires were included in the overall schedule, dealing with attitudes to a number of general issues, and the reciprocal attitudes of management and workforce towards each other.

The interview schedule used was derived from a pilot study carried out amongst technical staff working in two Scottish institutes of higher education. A copy of the complete schedule and questionnaires is given in the report *Alcohol and Work* (Davies, Cochrane and Marini, 1977–8).

The aim was to solicit the co-operation of five Glasgow firms/ employers, preferably including one which employed mainly white-collar (non-manual) workers. Since there is convincing evidence that alcoholism can occur at all levels of employment, it was decided to conduct interviews with employees from all levels, i.e. from shop-floor to top management. To facilitate comparison of total mean consumption figures between the different firms, the sample from each firm was structured in such a way that the number of workers at each level of employment in the firm, expressed as a percentage of the total workforce, would account for the same percentage of the sample from that firm. Sex was treated in the same way. In actual fact, the sample obtained failed to meet these specifications, since in some of the firms visited substantial numbers refused to take part or else simply failed to turn up for the interview. This means that comparisons between firms can only be made *within* a given level of employment.

Firms were initially contacted by sending two letters to an appropriate individual in the firm. The Scottish Council on Alcoholism sent a general introductory letter, outlining in broad terms the problem of alcohol abuse in industry, and the general aims and need for a study of the present type. This was accompanied by a letter from the Senior Employment Medical Officer for Scotland expressing support for the work and recommending it to the attention of the firm in question. If these initial contacts met with a favourable response, the firm was contacted by the University of Strathclyde and a meeting arranged at which the precise nature of the study, and its requirements, could be spelled out.

If initial discussions proved satisfactory on both sides, the co-operation of the appropriate trades unions was sought. In most cases, union representatives organised meetings to consider the issue of participation. If all concerned were happy that the project could go ahead, individual members of the workforce were selected randomly from computer lists of personnel (identified by number only), according to the sampling procedure described. Those selected were contacted individually by letter. The letter gave a brief description of the aims of the study, expressed the hope that the individual would be willing to take part, and gave a specific time (during working hours) and place (in the factory) where the interview would take place. No pressure was brought to bear on individuals who failed to turn up.

In order to secure co-operation from five major employers, it proved necessary to contact thirteen firms/organisations. These were:

(1) a book publisher
(2) a shipyard
(3) a construction/demolition firm 'a'
(4) a construction/demolition firm 'b'
(5) a vehicle manufacturer
(6) an engine/propulsion unit manufacturer
(7) a broadcasting organisation
(8) a sewing-machine manufacturer
(9) a government agency
(10) a regional council department
(11) a brewery
(12) a pump manufacturer
(13) a heavy engineering works.

Eight of these firms did not wish to participate, for a number of reasons. A description of the sample and response rate from the five firms who took part is given in Table 3.1. The variation in the number sampled reflects to some extent differing degrees of enthusiasm and tolerance from the different firms. In addition, low response rates within firms visited at the beginning of the project, particularly the engine/propulsion unit manufacturer, suggested the need for larger samples to be drawn in the future. The female response in the shipyard and the vehicle manufacturing company was extremely poor, and no account is taken of these cases in the individual analyses of these firms. The overall interview success rate (55.0 per cent of those sampled) is moderate rather than good. It seems likely that among those who failed to turn up there might be a number of heavy drinkers who did not wish to be interviewed. Problems of estimating prevalence

Table 3.1: Patterns of Response in the Five Companies

Type of firm	Total no. employed	No. sampled	No. of interviews obtained	Overall success rate (%)
Shipyard	5,500	300	148 (143m, 5f)	49.3
Regional Council Department	7,000	160	160 (72m, 88f)	100*
Vehicle manufacturer	8,800	150	81 (79m, 2f)	54
Engine/propulsion unit manufacturer	5,650	220	76 (63m, 13f)	34.5
Brewery	750	200	110 (84m, 26f)	55.5

(m = male, f = female)
*Due to low response rate, a different contact procedure was employed with this
  organisation.

of drinking in surveys have been discussed by Plant (1979a).

All interviews took place between late July and early December,
1977. Results are thus not contaminated by Christmas or New Year
celebrations.

Basic Consumption Data

Data on personal consumption were collected by asking each respondent
to think back to the last occasion on which he/she had had a drink. This
occasion was then recalled in detail, step by step, including details of
the place, the company, and the drinks consumed. Experience has
shown that better data are obtained when specific details of a specific
occasion are called for, than when some vague general question (such
as 'How much would you say you usually drink, on average?') is asked.
These latter tend to produce vague and general answers (e.g. 'About
average' or 'Just a couple of pints or so'). The respondent was then
asked how many times during the previous week he/she had been for a
drink. Then, using a system of equivalents to equate the different
alcohol contents of the beverages consumed, the data were combined
to produce a quantity/frequency type drinking score for each
individual. Tables 3.2 and 3.3 give the average drinking score for five

Table 3.2: Average Alcohol Consumption* for Occupational Group and Company (Males)

	1	2	3	4	5	Job classification
	single case	15 (9)	20.1 (71)	21.9 (38)	20.8 (24)	Shipyard
Mean alcohol units consumed	7.8 (27)	10.6 (38)	two cases	three cases	two cases	Regional Council Department
	single case	15.6 (20)	6.7 (17)	22.1 (16)	29 (25)	Vehicle manufacturer
	4.8 (4)	10.5 (12)	21 (30)	22 (7)	11.2 (10)	Engine/propulsion unit manufacturer
	17.4 (7)	11 (5)	27.9 (22)	16.2 (23)	52 (27)	Brewery
n =	40	84	142	87	88	
Total alc. units	352	1031	2813	1962	2746	
Overall mean alc. units	9.25	12.3	19.8	22.5	31.2	

(Numbers in brackets indicate number in each cell.)
*Consumption is in units of alcohol (1 unit = either ½ pint of beer, lager, cider, etc. or a single glass of wine or spirits.)

Table 3.3: Average Alcohol Consumption* for Occupational Group and Company (Females)

	1	2	3	4	5	Job classification
	3.5 (21)	4.5 (31)	3.7 (13)	3.4 (11)	5.2 (12)	Regional Council Department
Mean alcohol units consumed	0 (0)	0 (0)	single case	4.7 (6)	11.2 (6)	Engine/propulsion unit manufacturer
	0 (0)	two cases	4.8 (5)	3.8 (6)	14.2 (13)	Brewery
n =	21	33	19	23	31	
Total alc. units	73	146	72	88	314	
Overall mean alc. units	3.5	4.4	4	3.8	10.1	

(Numbers in brackets indicate number in each cell.)
*Consumption is in units of alcohol.

different occupational status groups (according to the Registrar General's classification of jobs and occupations) for each of the five firms who participated.

A word of caution is necessary about the data in Tables 3.2 and 3.3. First, mean drinking scores can be misleading since the distribution of drinking scores in a population is not normal, but has a long 'tail'. Consequently means can give a distorted impression of what 'normal' drinking entails, in terms of both mode and distribution. In the report *Alcohol and Work* (Davies, Cochrane and Marini, 1977–8) from which these data are derived, graphs are supplied to give the precise nature of the distribution of drinking scores; alternative scoring systems are used in deriving drinking categories; and log conversion scales used whenever raw scores are used in computations. Pressure on space prevents a full account of these precautions being given in this chapter. Finally, the reader will observe that cell totals for some occupational groups in particular firms are low, rendering the mean for that cell unreliable. Results for individual firms should thus be viewed with caution in these instances.

Although the inadequacies of mean scores are considerable, the simple data in Tables 3.2 and 3.3 serve as a basis for some broad generalisations. First, for the males, an increase in consumption is observed in progressing from class one to class five, when overall class means are calculated; though there were instances of heavy drinking in all classes. For the females, class-five workers again appear to drink more than other class groups, though the trend is less uniform. (Women readers may be interested to note that in all cases except the Regional Council Department, which is non-manufacturing, few women were employed in class one or class two occupations.) In all instances, class-five women drank significantly[1] more than the others; though interestingly, there was a very slight tendency for upwardly-mobile females to drink more than females who displayed no job mobility or who were downwardly mobile in the Regional Council Department.

There are some marked differences between firms for people in a given class group, which may be illustrated by Tables 3.2 and 3.3. In particular, the data from the male class-five brewery workers are of special interest, and can be compared with findings from Plant (1979a). Plant's study showed that alcohol production workers, especially those in manual jobs, drank more heavily on average than workers in another manufacturing industry. The study examined new recruits to the drink trade, and concluded that the alcohol production industry

attracted heavy drinkers, rather than creating them. For those in
manual jobs in the alcohol production industry, a self-reported consumption figure of 33.13 alcohol units per week was reported. In the
present study the comparable figure is 34.1 units per week, which
is very close to Plant's figure and attests to the reliability of the
symbolic answers obtained. In the present study, the consumption of
the unskilled manual workers (Social Class 5) is worth some further
comment. For this group, average weekly consumption of 52 units
was reported, an amount considerably in excess of any other group.
In this industry, but also in some of the others, there were individual
reports of quite spectacular consumption; though such consumption
is not *typical* of any group. Dight's recent study (1976) suggests that
in Scotland, one third of all the alcohol consumed is drunk by only
three per cent (mostly males) of the population. Finally, in terms of
the scoring system used, the incidence of 'heavy drinking' appeared
to be lowest in the Regional Council Department, which employed
a substantial number of women and few male manual workers (classes
four and five) and also in the engine/propulsion unit manufacturer,
though in this latter case there might have been more defensiveness
than usual. More precise comparison of raw consumption figures for
different firms is unwise in view of sample inadequacies.

Dight's study found that the heaviest drinkers were young males
in class five occupations. The data from the present study show some
tendency to heavier drinking among the lower socio-economic class
males, but the data with respect to age are not uniform. For male
workers, those employed with the vehicle manufacturer, the Regional
Council Department and the engine/propulsion unit manufacturer
tended to show heavier drinking amongst the younger males; but this
was not the case in the shipyard or the brewery. For females, a similar
slight relationship was found in the Regional Council Department
and the engine/propulsion unit manufacturer, but not in the brewery.

Although these associations are slight, no evidence was found to
support an opposite hypothesis (i.e. that older workers drank more
than younger ones); thus whenever evidence for a relationship
between age and consumption was found, it showed higher consumption amongst the younger workers. It is interesting to speculate about
the failure of this relationship to emerge in the shipyard and the
brewery. It might be the case that certain industries employ a manual
workforce amongst which the consumption of substantial amounts
of alcohol is normal throughout a large age range, perhaps as a
response to certain aspects of the work offered. The way in which

Table 3.4: Percentages of Males and Females in Each Company Who Reported Lunchtime Drinking in Week Preceding Interview (Weekends Excluded)

	Males	Females
Shipyard	28% (143)	—
Regional Council Department	25% (72)	15% (88)
Vehicle manufacturer	51% (79)	—
Engine/propulsion unit manufacturer	25% (63)	0% (13)
Brewery	71% (84)	42% (26)

(Numbers in brackets indicate number in each cell.)

alcohol production attracts heavy drinkers has already been mentioned. Similar selective factors may operate in other industries, for a number of reasons.

In addition to the basic drinking data referred to in the above paragraphs, information was separately obtained about alcohol consumption during the working day. In the main, heavy overall consumption was associated with heavy lunchtime drinking. (There were exceptions. Not all heavy drinkers drank at lunchtimes and in addition there was a small group of individuals who drank at lunchtime but not in the evenings. This is an atypical pattern which might merit future study.) In Table 3.4, the percentages of men and women in each firm who took a drink at lunchtime during the week preceding the interview are given. Whilst some of these percentages are substantial, there is no indication in *these* figures of the quantities consumed, and consequently they do not necessarily indicate excessive consumption, or even consumption likely to affect work performance. In terms of actual quantities consumed, the heaviest lunchtime drinking was reported in the brewery and the vehicle factory. Only in these two firms did the lunchtime consumption exceed 50 alcohol units for any individual during the previous week. (This is equivalent to about five pints of beer/lager or ten whiskies per lunchtime each working day.) For the vehicle manufacturer, four individuals (about five per cent of those interviewed in this factory, or ten per cent of those who

drank at lunchtime from this firm) exceeded 50 alcohol units per week
in lunchtime drinking alone. *If* this rate is characteristic for the total
workforce of 8,800, there would be about 445 individuals in the firm
exceeding this amount. The heaviest-drinking lunchtime drinker in this
firm had a consumption equivalent to about 6.5 pints of beer or 13
single shots of spirits per lunchtime. In the brewery, six individuals
exceeded 50 lunchtime alcohol units (seven per cent of those interviewed or roughtly ten per cent of those who drank at lunchtime).
This rate, *if* general, would produce 54 individuals in excess of 50
units per week, out of the workforce of 750. Overall, the brewery had
the highest proportion of lunchtime drinkers. Lunchtime drinking
was reported the least in the engine manufacturer and the Regional
Council Department, with the shipyard somewhere in between.

In addition to the preceding questions, respondents were also asked
if they knew of any occasions on which alcohol was brought onto the
premises, or consumed during working hours. This is a sensitive
question, since in four of the firms visited this is specifically against
company regulations. In the brewery, 90 per cent of those interviewed reported that they were aware that this took place. The
equivalent percentage in the shipyard was 64 per cent with the other
firms somewhere between these values. There is little doubt that such
knowledge is widespread. More specifically, 64 per cent of the males
interviewed in the brewery *personally* admitted consuming alcohol
during working hours; so did 20 per cent in the shipyard, 11 per cent
in the engine/propulsion unit manufacturer, and nine per cent in the
vehicle factory. There were no such admissions in the Regional Council
Department. For female workers, the percentages were all very low
(eight per cent or less) except in the brewery where 34 per cent
answered this question in the affirmative. (In the opinion of the
author, at least part of the difference between the brewery and the
other firms is due to the openness and candour with which alcohol
and drink problems could be discussed, at all levels, in this firm.)

Reports of Drink-related Incidents

The people interviewed were asked to express opinions about the
effects of alcohol upon work performance in the factory where they
worked, and also to describe any alcohol-related incidents of which
they had knowledge. In the brewery, the shipyard and the Regional
Council Department, the most frequently-expressed opinion was that

alcohol had no effect upon work performance. In the vehicle manufacturer and the engine/propulsion unit factory, however, the most
frequent opinion was that the quality of work was definitely impaired
by alcohol consumption. (Percentages of males in the sample, in each
firm, reporting impairment, were as follows: brewery 18 per cent,
shipyard 18 per cent, Regional Council 12.5 per cent, vehicle manufacturer 39 per cent, engine/propulsion unit manufacturer 30 per
cent.) In considering these figures, it is worthwhile bearing in mind
that alcohol consumption was apparently lowest in the Council
Department, which might account for the low figures from there;
and also that of the remaining firms, the shipyard and the brewery
make less use of highly-skilled labour than the other two firms. It
might be the case that drinking really does interfere more seriously,
or more rapidly, with the performance of skilled jobs than with
unskilled jobs. Other frequently-mentioned effects were tiredness
and sluggishness. Very few respondents spontaneously mentioned
absenteeism or accidents in connection with alcohol consumption.

With respect to drunkenness at work, respondents in all firms
except the Regional Council Department reported a high frequency
of knowledge of occasions on which someone had been 'drunk'
whilst at work. The percentage of males and females giving such
reports was between 73 per cent and 80 per cent in all these firms.
In the Regional Council, the percentage was lower at 25 per cent.
The data do not indicate whether the widespread knowledge of
drunkenness incidents comes from many cases, or from a few highly
visible ones. With regard to accidents in which alcohol might have been
involved, the data are if anything weaker. These are very sensitive
topics, and without doubt produce defensive reactions of varying
degrees in many respondents. For accidents, the shipyard, the brewery
and the vehicle manufacturer gave results which were almost identical.
The percentage of those males interviewed who affirmed that they
had knowledge of alcohol-related accidents was 21 per cent in all
cases. In the engine/propulsion unit company and the Regional
Council Department, eleven per cent and three per cent of males
respectively gave this answer. The occurrence of positive answers
from females was very low (eight per cent or less). The most frequent
types of alcohol-related accidents reported were those involving
machinery, and those involving falls of various kinds. The low rate
in the Regional Council Department may again reflect the generally
low reported consumption, but is in part possibly due also to the
fact that it is harder to have accidents sitting behind a desk than

when engaged in more active work. Whilst the shipyard is not unique with respect to accidents, it is of interest that the shipyard group newspaper ran a front page headline story entitled 'You're Slipping' during the period when the interviews were taking place. The article dealt with the large number of accidents occurring in the yard. Most of these were apparently falls, involving such things as 'tripping over hoses', 'disappearing down open manholes' and 'sliding down ladders'. Some of the falls were described as 'tragically funny'. 'A stranger to the yard,' continued the article, 'could be forgiven for thinking he was reading the script for a clip from Keystone Cops.' The article stated that there were 1,176 non-reportable accidents during the month of July, accounting for 356 man-days lost, at a cost of £52,860. However, no mention of alcohol was made anywhere in the report.

The subject areas dealt with in the paragraphs immediately preceding are very sensitive topics, dealing as they do with behaviours which obviously contravene company regulations in some instances. The data are weak, and may shed more light on people's defensiveness than upon actual rates of occurrence in the different firms. The information in these paragraphs is best viewed as impressionistic, and as a source of questions and hypotheses.

Data Provided by Firms

The firms which took part in the study were asked if they would provide certain data from their own records which might cast light on absenteeism, wastage rates, accidents and dismissals, especially where these might be alcohol-related. Because of problems of retrieval and the lack of detail in records, certain of this information could not be provided. The engine manufacturer and the Regional Council Department were unable to provide data of any kind on these issues. The shipyard could provide only minimal information. The brewery and the vehicle manufacturer, however, provided as much of this information as possible.

The shipyard could provide only minimal data, plus some impressionistic material. For hourly-paid workers, authorised and unauthorised absenteeism accounted for 13 per cent of the man-days lost per year. No figures were available for salaried staff. Over a one-year period, there were 7,450 reportable accidents, but these figures were not broken down by day of the week. Impressionistic reports suggested that instances of heavy drinking at work were regular occurrences.

The vehicle manufacturer could provide fuller information. In a six-month period, there were eleven alcohol-related dismissals, and ten alcohol-related final warnings. These are actions of last resort, indicating that other workers who have alcohol problems exist in the firm, but that these courses of action had not thus far extended to them. Absenteeism differed significantly on different days of the week though there was no difference between direct and indirect labour in respect of absenteeism. Absenteeism was highest at the beginning (Monday) of the week, but accidents were most frequent when absenteeism was lowest. This might be because the more people there are present, the more people there are to have accidents Weekend hangovers might contribute to the Monday absence figures

Fairly full data were also provided by the brewery, though again more information was available for non-salaried (hourly-paid) than for salaried workers. No data could be provided for alcohol-related dismissals, though the company had referred six individuals to the Scottish Council on Alcoholism during 1977. Reportable accidents were logged in an 'accident book'. Accidents involving 'carelessness' and 'equipment/ machinery' accounted for 73 per cent of the accidents reported. No separate category for 'alcohol-related accidents' was used, but it seems likely that alcohol-related accidents would contribute mostly to the two categories outlined above. Data were provided for authorised and unauthorised (no sick-note) absenteeism. Unauthorised absenteeism was typically of about one day's duration, whilst authorised absence was for longer periods (mean, nine days). In any month, an average of 46 per cent of the number absent are 'unauthorised'. Accidents seem more likely to occur when authorised absence is high, rather than when unauthorised absence is high. Unauthorised absence is highest at the beginning of the week; this is not the case for authorised absence. Speculatively, it seems likely that weekend hangovers would contribute to the Monday unauthorised absence figures.

Drink-related Attitudes and Opinions

The study, from which the above findings are a selection, contains a good deal of data on the relationships between drinking and certain attitudes. Some of these findings are relevant to the issue of alcoholism *generally*, rather than of specific interest to those concerned

with problems of alcohol at work. Alcoholism has roots which go
beyond the immediate work environment, so the study of these
broader issues is of considerable importance. In the present context
however, where the main issue concerns the practical problems of
the work environment, a full description of drink and attitude
relationships may be out of place.

Nonetheless, certain of the findings in this category are of relevance
to the work situation. Previous studies of young people's drinking
behaviour, e.g. Aitken (1978) and Davies and Stacey (1972), have
shown that young teenagers and adolescents who drink more than
normal amounts (by comparison with others of their own age group)
tend to have particular views on certain subjects. For example, many
of them believe that drinking alcohol bestows on the drinker a number
of properties, including greater sexual attractiveness, toughness, an
aura of maturity, greater sociability, and the ability to 'look after
yourself'. Being able to 'hold your drink' is seen as a virtue and a sign
of manliness. Using similar techniques, it was found in the present
study that heavier-drinking adults often tended also to endorse these
beliefs. It has sometimes been assumed that such attitudes are
'juvenile' or 'immature' in so far as they are subscribed to by
youngsters; the present study shows, however, that such a description
is sometimes inappropriate since many adults apparently share similar
beliefs too. In so far as certain types of health propaganda have been
aimed specifically at young people, with the aim of reshaping stereo-
typed views such as those described above, the finding that certain
views are shared by adults, especially those in the heavier-drinking
groups, suggests a need for a similar type of propaganda aimed at
more adult audiences. It may be that certain aspects of the work
situation and environment might provide appropriate contexts for
the dissemination of such messages.

A related issue concerns the people in firms who might best lead
any alcohol education campaign. One facet of the present study is of
special interest from this point of view. At one point during the
interview, members of the lower workforce were asked to fill in a
questionnaire to describe those people who worked in managerial
posts. Those working in managerial positions were, in turn, asked to
fill in a questionnaire to describe the lower workforce. A full description of the methods used to produce the questionnaire, and the
data analysis, is given in the original report and in Davies (1978).It
appears that people answered the questionnaire in terms of three
underlying dimensions or 'factors', concerning respectively:

sociability at work; achievement and the desire to 'get on'; and tough-ness. When respondents' answers were examined in the light of their own drinking behaviour, some interesting and important differences emerged. In general terms, amongst both management and lower workforce, the heavier drinkers tended to rate their opposite numbers as more 'work sociable'; that is, heavier-drinking members of the work-force rated managers as higher on this factor, and heavier-drinking managers rated the workforce as higher also. High scores on this factor involved items like 'honest', 'hardworking', 'friendly', 'helpful' and 'bright'. By contrast, low scores involved items like 'lazy', 'unfriendly', 'unhelpful', 'deceitful' and 'dim'. Amongst both manage-ment and workforce, the heavier drinkers made more positive evaluations; but in addition, those drinking less tended to use the negative aspects more frequently. In the present sample, the small number of abstinent managers made by far the most negative evaluations of the lower workforce; such low scores were not produced by any other section of the sample.

In terms of the 'ambitious' factor, although there were differences between those who drank to differing degrees, the most striking aspect of the results was a tendency (perhaps understandable) for those amongst the lower workforce to rate managers as having 'achievement motivation' in terms of the questionnaire; and perhaps more surprisingly, the general tendency for managers to rate the lower workforce as 'satisfied'.

Finally, in terms of the 'toughness' factor, important differences again emerged between managers and lower-workforce members who drank to differing extents. Most managers rated the lower workforce as 'tough' to some degree, with the abstinent and light-drinking managers seeing them as most tough. By contrast, only the heavy-drinking managers rated the lower workforce as 'not so tough'. In a similar kind of way, there were differences between the judgements about management made by lower workforce members who drank to different degrees. Overall, the lower workforce made fewer 'tough' judgements about management, than did management about the lower workforce. Once again, however, it was the lighter drinkers in both groups who tended to make the most 'tough' judgements, and the heavier drinkers who made the most 'not so tough' judgements. Heavy-drinking members of the management and of the lower workforce resembled each other in rating each other as 'not so tough'.

From the point of view of alcohol campaigns in industry, the above findings and especially those concerning work sociability might have some important implications. First, the dispelling of myths about alcohol consumption is an important facet of adult, and not merely of child or youth-oriented, campaigns. Secondly, if it is decided to recruit members of management to lead, or act as figureheads for, alcohol campaigns in industry, it seems advisable to select individuals for this role who have the most positive views of the lower workforce. On the basis of the present data, it seems that in many instances such a person is likely to be himself a heavy drinker, and that by contrast certain abstainers may have relatively unfavourable views.

Finally, in the present study, there was a tendency for the heavier drinkers to have more extreme views of the 'typical alcoholic' in terms of a 'skid-row' stereotype. The dispelling of this view, and the re-instatement in its place of the fact that one does not have to be on skid-row to encounter serious drink problems, may be of particular relevance for both managers and workers who fall in the target group.

Discussion

It is worth repeating that the results obtained in the present study are obtained from a sample which is not completely satisfactory. In a study of the present type it is difficult to deal with this problem since individuals cannot be coerced into revealing details about themselves if they do not wish to do so. There are clearly difficulties in obtaining data, and these difficulties are likely to recur in studies conducted along the present lines. It is apparent that drawing balanced and representative samples is to little avail where highly-sensitive topics are concerned, in circumstances where substantial numbers of individuals can easily avoid taking part after the sample has been drawn. These problems do not mean that findings are necessarily invalid, but rather that their validity is uncertain. Consequently, further support for findings, from independent sources, is required. Credence is given to the data however by the finding of systematic differences between drinking groups, and the support obtained for relationships and differences which have been found in studies with better samples. It is not unreasonable therefore to make some general statements about the data from this study, with the proviso that in some cases, further supportive evidence is needed.

Previous studies have shown relationships between drinking and social class. In the present study, this relationship (see Table 3.2) is also supported. In so far as some firms draw substantial proportions of their manual workforce from amongst the lowest group, in which heavy drinking is possibly more widespread, the occurrence of alcohol problems is to be expected, indeed anticipated. It is unreasonable to recruit large numbers of workers from amongst a social group in which heavy drinking is, for some members, a *norm*, and expect not to encounter the effects normally associated with it. In four of the five firms which participated in this study, there is a formal policy prohibiting alcohol consumption on the premises. This policy is understandable, since in three of the firms, lives will eventually depend on the final product. However, rather more is required from firms in the way of an *active* positive policy towards alcohol problems. Clearly, there are two sides to this problem, and no simple answer. However, discussion of these issues is urgently required, since there may be a logical dilemma in a situation where there are two conflicting sets of rules, i.e. one set which prohibits alcohol consumption at pain of disciplinary action, up to and including dismissal, and another set which offers help to those with alcohol problems.

There were large differences between firms in their ability to provide data about disciplinary action with respect to alcohol. The vehicle manufacturer and the brewery provided the best data. Minimal data were also obtained from the shipyard. The engine propulsion unit manufacturer and Regional Council could provide no data on this matter. Some senior members of firms outlined policies on alcohol problems, including such things as referring employees with alcohol problems to counselling or therapeutic agencies, keeping an alcoholic employee's job open for a period while he/she undergoes treatment, and placing a newly returned 'patient' to work alongside an ex-alcoholic employee for moral support. Whilst there was tangible evidence of a real operational policy of some kind in two of the firms, this was not uniformly the case. There was a suspicion, possibly unfounded, that sometimes there might be a discrepancy between the 'official' alcohol policy and the way the system actually worked (for example, in cases where channels apparently existed for referral, but which were hardly ever used). It is not always possible for research workers to distinguish between a real operational policy, and one which exists in theory but seldom in practice. Whatever the realities of the situations existing in the different firms, there is no doubt that each year individuals *can* and *do* lose their jobs through drink; so the dismissal threat is not purely an idle one.

In so far as different firms have different problems, different attitudes towards alcoholism, and different needs, it seems likely that any organisation trying to introduce alcohol education 'packages' into firms would do well to take these differences into account, and tailor particular packages to particular firms. The acceptability and usefulness of a standard set of alcohol education procedures is likely to be variable between firms. Differences between personalities, and different views of alcoholism, may also affect the way in which health propaganda is presented and consequently received. The findings with respect to management and worker views are of interest since, if this state of affairs is general, there is likely to be a better chance of success when heavy drinkers in management are associated with the propaganda. This is not to imply that confirmed teetotallers are necessarily the wrong people to lead campaigns, but rather that there are advantages in involving drinkers as well. Perhaps industrial alcoholism programs sacrifice credibility if they are seen to be led mainly by people who do not drink.

In the present study, a small number of employees had a strong dislike of their jobs, professed to having few outside interests and hobbies, and described their jobs as boring and repetitive. These kinds of reports, whilst not particularly widespread, came more frequently from heavy drinkers. The hypothesis is suggested that *some* drinking might be a reaction to an unsatisfying kind of life. (There are, of course, other possible hypotheses.) It is suggested that a comprehensive approach to the problems of alcohol in employment must look not simply at people with alcohol problems, but also at the jobs they are asked to do. The notion that the problem can be 'cured' by means which involve firms only in action directed to individuals, and not involving some critical appraisal of the formal and *informal* systems and norms which prevail in the factory itself, is naive.

In conclusion, some points arising from the general conduct of the study, and not necessarily related to the data obtained, are outlined in the remaining paragraphs. These issues seem important, though the reader may disagree with the individual interpretation placed on them in some instances.

In some of the firms where the study was conducted, data on such things as attendance/absenteeism, disciplinary action, and certain other categories of behaviour were available only for hourly-paid workers and not for salaried employees. It is not suggested here that this represents any deliberate discriminatory policy. Rather, it appears that the situation arises mainly for logistical reasons, or perhaps through simple default. Nonetheless, there are two unfortunate consequences.

First, the missing data make comparisons of different sections of the workforce impossible with respect to particular aspects of job performance. Secondly, the possibility exists that such a state of affairs might be *perceived* as discriminatory, and might reinforce any tendency to believe that problems at the management level are treated differently from those amongst the lower workforce. With such a sensitive topic as alcoholism, it is perhaps important that equality of treatment is seen to exist at all levels.

Attempts to focus attention on the problems of alcohol abuse/ alcoholism in industry frequently make use of the economic argument. The cost to the total economy is frequently stressed, sometimes to the exclusion of costs (economic or otherwise) to the individual. An illustration of the point can be taken from a conference on the topic of alcohol abuse in industry which was attended by the author. A number of telling phrases were repeatedly used by speakers, and appeared to meet with general approval. Examples are: 'firms are not in business for fun'; 'firms after all are in business to make a profit'; and 'we must be realistic'. These types of phrases, when analysed closely, have some unfortunate implications. The first statement implies that any attempt to tackle the industrial alcohol problem which is not soundly based on economic necessities is trivial, or 'fun'. The second phrase implies that a firm's sole consideration is with making a profit, and that other functions and responsibilities are at best of secondary importance. With respect to the third type of phrase, the author is of the opinion that the word 'realistic' is frequently used euphemistically in the hope that someone will thereby be absolved from certain 'unrealistic' courses of action which involve immediate economic cost rather than profit. There is nothing especially 'realistic' about this view; and the possible implication that non-profit-making interventions on behalf of employed alcoholics are 'unrealistic' is rather worrying. A perfectly reasonable alternative view is that firms and organisations have duties and responsibilities towards alcoholic people in their employ, whether or not these in themselves prove economically profitable. A related issue concerns the argument that sacking drunkenness offenders is economically wasteful, and especially so where the loss of skilled labour might mean the loss of training investment. This argument is again not an entirely happy one, since if cirumstances change, proponents of the economic argument must logically recommend the opposite course of action, or have their bluff called. Finally on this point, some firms take their social responsibilities quite seriously, and the overstressing of the economic arguments does them less than justice.

A related point concerns the use of 'estimates' of the cost to the economy to bolster arguments about the need for action on the problem of alcohol in industry. Over the last few years, a number of such 'estimates' have been 'calculated'. Typically these sums range from somewhere around £88 million up to about £350 million per annum.[2] The richness and variety of some of these estimates is sufficient to arouse suspicion. Since an almost limitless number of factors may be seen as contributing to these figures, they may often reflect the creativity of the accountant rather than any precise view of reality. The things included in estimates are rarely made explicit, so the figures remain meaningless. In addition, the use of non-legitimate averaging can produce some amazing results which have no statistical validity. (For example if a man works eight hours out of every 24, he works one-third of the time available. There are 365 days in a year so he contributes about 122 days labour per year. However, he takes off 52 weekends, or 104 days, leaving 18 days labour. Then he takes off a further fortnight for holidays, leaving four days. If he then takes off the odd couple of days for bank holidays, and a couple more for whatever reason, we can demonstrate that the average working man never actually does any work at all.) By changing the averaging base from the 'average firm' to the economy as a whole, or in the opposite direction to the individual employee, some startling results can be obtained. These estimates sometimes represent the misuse of statistics and very little else; and unfortunately the reader of such statistical conclusions has no way of discriminating between more-reliable and less-reliable estimates. Viewed in this kind of way, the cost is probably very great, but it seems unwise to put spuriously exact figures on it.

There is, however, another way of viewing the 'cost' to the economy, which is arguably fairer and more balanced; namely, in the context of the *contribution* of alcohol sales to the economy. In 1972, the Medical Council on Alcoholism Ltd calculated, in an apparently straightforward manner, that the government received somewhere in the region of £1500 million in revenue from the liquor industry. In the same year, they 'estimated' the cost of alcohol abuse to industry as possibly 'over £100 millions'. Overall, therefore (given the variability of such estimates) one might conclude *not* that alcohol cost the country £100 million, but that it contributed £1400 million. To separate the cost of alcohol abuse from the contribution of alcohol sales is to be highly selective, more so when there exists scientific evidence that, at the very least, there is some degree of association between the overall *per capita* consumption in a population, and the proportion of that population who are likely to drink excessively (Ledermann, 1956; Davies, 1978). The selective use of statistics to bolster a particular viewpoint or position is a well-known political device. It is also an extremely flexible one. Whilst it would admittedly be silly and unjust to do so, one could calculate the cost of *abstinence* to the economy if one so desired (with apologies it appears, for example, that abstainers 'cost' the economy in excess of £28 million[3] *per annum* by failing to drink whisky alone. This 'estimate' is derived by calculating the average contribution of drinkers to the total excise tax derived from proof gallons of whisky, and multiplying by the estimated number of abstainers in the population.) In other words, the derivation and use of 'cost' estimates is selectively biased, and whether such bias is legitimate in this context is a matter for debate.

The above arguments lose much of their force when the economic argument for intervention is given less prominence. Initially, economics looks like a good basis for persuading firms to adopt more humane policies on alcoholism, since it is assumed that this is the kind of message most likely to appeal to businessmen. However, the attribution to businessmen of motives which are entirely economic, whether true or not, is unfortunate. As Andreski (1974) writes, 'By foisting on people a certain image of themselves, we make them live up to it.' Economics in the longer term might prove a fickle and rather fragile mistress, compared to more durable motives for behaviour. As a nation we make at least some attempt to look after the sick, the injured, the aged, and others in need of help; most people would agree that there is a social obligation and a moral duty to do so. It is not clear, therefore, why the treatment of alcoholics in a particular sector has to be shown to be a profitable enterprise.

Acknowledgement

Funds for the execution of the study upon which this chapter is based were obtained by the Scottish Council on Alcoholism and provided by the Manpower Services Commission, to whom thanks are due.

Notes

1. In order to simplify presentation, statistical tests are not included in this chapter. Whenever 'significant' differences are mentioned, this indicates that statistical tests indicated at least a 95 per cent probability of differences ($p < 0.05$).

2. In view of the nature of the argument at this point, it would perhaps be unfair to give a more precise list of 'estimates' and the bodies associated with them.

3. There is no reason to believe that this estimate is any less dubious than any of the others referred to in this section.

4 THE MEDICAL PROFESSION

Robin M. Murray

The frequency of alcohol dependence in members of the medical profession and the consequent potential for harm to both doctors and their patients has attracted a great deal of comment recently (Symposium, 1978). But only too often this debate has proceeded without reference to available information on the general health of doctors. For instance, it is often assumed that because of long hours of work, close contact with disease, or some particular stress of medicine, doctors suffer increased physical illness. But, statistics published in Britain by the Office of Population Censuses and Surveys (Office of Population Censuses and Surveys, 1978) demonstrate that, on the contrary, doctors have a greater than average life-expectancy. These statistics used as a measure of longevity the Standard Mortality Ratio (SMR), which is the ratio of observed deaths in a population divided by those expected from the national death rates, standardised for age and sex, and multiplied by 100. The latest figures show that doctors have an overall SMR of 81 — that is their life-expectancy is 19 per cent greater than that of the general population. American studies have reached similar conclusions (Williams *et al.*, 1971).

It would have been pleasant to be able to report that this increased survival is a consequence of doctors' particular knowledge of health risks and their resultant healthier lifestyle. That this is not a major influence is shown by the fact that other members of Social Class 1 do even better than doctors — their SMR is 77. It appears that much of doctors' increased survival can be attributed to the highly selective procedure that admits primarily healthy individuals from the middle and upper social classes to medical school (Williams *et al.*, 1971). Thereafter, members of the profession have the benefits of high socio-economic status and direct access to competent and, if necessary, highly-specialised medical care. The only health hazard which doctors have consciously avoided with benefit to their health appears to be cigarette smoking. In 1951, the cigarette consumption of British male doctors was similar to the national average, but by 1971 it had fallen to between one-quarter and one-half of that of the general population (Doll and Pete, 1976), and the SMR for doctors from lung cancer was 33 per cent of that expected (Office of

61

Population Censuses and Surveys, 1978).

Psychological Health of Doctors

There are only three major conditions from which doctors are more likely to die than the general population (Office of Population Censuses and Surveys, 1978). These and their respective SMRs are suicide (335 per cent), cirrhosis (311 per cent) and accidents (180 per cent). Since at least two of these have psychological origins, interest has turned from the physical to the mental health of doctors. Indeed, the mental health of doctors has been more extensively researched than that of any other occupational group. This is partly because of concern over the damage that mentally-ill doctors may do to their patients, but also reflects the fact that doctors who have carried out the majority of psychiatric research, are especially interested in the mental health of members of their own profession.

One method of obtaining information about doctors' mental health is to study doctors treated for mental illness, and in the past 14 years seven major series of such doctors have been published. These are summarised in Table 4.1. The doctor-patients who were studied came from three different types of institution — private hospitals, teaching hospitals, and the personal clinics of well-known professors. These are all likely to have preferentially attracted sick doctors, which may explain the over-representation of doctors in their patient populations, and also why the authors became interested in the problem. These series are not strictly comparable among themselves since some contain both inpatients and outpatients while others contain only inpatients. Nevertheless, there are interesting similarities, including the mean age of the doctor-patients, which ranged from only 42 to 54 years, and the rates of divorce and separation, which varied from only seven to 13 per cent.

In spite of differences in the diagnostic criteria employed, some trends in diagnosis emerge. Drug addiction and alcoholism were disturbingly common, and 51 per cent of the Mayo Clinic doctor-patients were addicted to drugs or alcohol. The percentage diagnosed as having affective psychosis ranged from 21 to 40 per cent, but the percentage considered to have a schizophrenic psychosis was only two to twelve per cent. (Small *et al.* (1969) used a category of 'schizophrenic reactions', which included non-psychotics.) Similarly, personality disorder and organic psychosis were relatively-seldom diagnosed.

	Duffy and Litin (1964)	a'Brook et al. (1967)	Vincent et al. (1969)	Pond (1969)	Small et al. (1969)	Franklin (1977)	Jones (1977)
Subjects	93 inpatients	192 inpatients and outpatients	93 inpatients	83 inpatients and outpatients	40 inpatients	100 inpatients	100 inpatients
Source	Mayo Clinic, USA	St Andrew's and Atkinson Morley Hospitals, and Prof Curran's private clinic, UK	Homewood Sanatorium, Canada	Maudsley and Priory Hospitals, and Prof Pond's private clinic, UK	Indiana Medical Center, USA	The Retreat, UK	Pennsylvania Hospital, USA
	%	%	%	%	%	%	%
Affective psychosis	21	28	14	28	15	40	24
Alcoholism		12	27	20	18	20	5
Drug dependence	51*	17	30	?	15	10	5
Neurosis	20	16	14	21	?	17	52
Schizophrenia	7	9	5	12	52†	2	6
Personality disorder	7	13	4	?	?	4	3
Organic psychosis	9	5	5	7	?	8	1

* Includes secondary diagnosis.
† Category of 'schizophrenic reactions'.

These results may have been distorted by the special position that doctors occupy in relation to psychiatric treatment. Not only can doctors treat themselves or seek psychiatric advice informally but, if they have a particular complaint, they may, because of their professional awareness, seek out a doctor or hospital with particular expertise in that condition. Consequently these studies cannot give accurate information about the frequency of different illnesses.

Pond (1969) appreciated this and, indeed, demonstrated considerable differences in the age, sex, occupational status and specialty pursued by doctors seen at the three institutions he studied (Maudsley Hospital, Priory Hospital and his personal clinic). Unfortunately, the authors of the other studies give no indication that they understood how potentially unrepresentative their patients might have been.

To obtain a more representative sample, Murray (1977) studied the admissions to and discharges from all Scottish psychiatric hospitals of male doctors over a ten-year period, and compared them with the figures for all non-medical Social Class 1 males. The overall mean annual first admission rate was 449 per 100,000 for male doctors, and 205 per 100,00 for non-medical Social Class 1 males. As can be seen in Figure 4.1 the doctors' rates were higher for all age groups.

The Causes of Psychiatric Disorder in Doctors

It is clear from the foregoing that doctors are, indeed, more likely to be admitted to psychiatric hospitals than their social and economic equals. But does this reflect increased prevalence of psychiatric disorder among doctors or is it merely an artefact produced by doctors' easier access to psychiatric care? Vaillant and his colleagues (Vaillant, Brighton and McArthur, 1970; Vaillant, Sobowale and McArthur, 1972) favoured the former explanation. Their investigation began over 30 years ago when 268 college sophomores were chosen on the basis of their good health and academic success to be studied intensively by a university health service. The assessments carried out at this time included ratings of their psychological stability and the quality of their childhood. By chance, 46 of these students went on to medical school, and these, plus 79 control students who did not, were followed up by questionnaire every two years for the next three decades. Doctors, especially those involved in direct patient care, were more likely than controls to report being unhappily-married, to

Figure 4.1: First Admission Rates to Scottish Psychiatric In-patient Beds of Male Doctors and Social Class 1 Controls

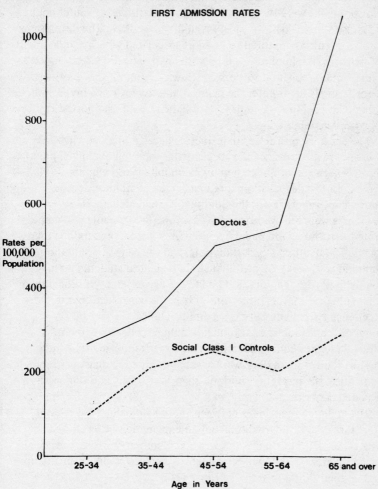

abuse drugs and to require to have psychiatric treatment.

Vaillant and his colleagues reported that the doctors who developed most problems were those with the most unsatisfactory childhoods, and those who had shown most instability at college. The development of life difficulties appeared to be more associated with maladjustment before medical school rather than with any particular stress related to medical practice. These authors conclude, therefore, that a vulnerable minority of students enter medicine as an attempt to be involved in caring relationships to compensate for their own unsupported child-hoods and instability.

The contrary position is that doctors have an increased liability to breakdown because of the special stress incurred in clinical practice. This has been forcefully argued by Cramond (1969) who used the Neuroticism Scale Questionnaire in a survey of all local doctors whose names appeared in the South Australian Medical Register. Responses were received from 810 doctors (54 per cent) and demon-strated that those who had care of patients were more anxious than non-clinical doctors, e.g. pathologists, and the general population. Cramond contrasted this with Australian medical students who, he claimed, were less anxious and had fewer psychiatric symptoms than other students; on this rather flimsy basis he concluded that doctors experience a rise in anxiety on assuming clinical responsibility. Cramond's questionnaire also included items concerning the most stressful areas of clinical practice. The doctors reported that their greatest sources of anxiety were therapeutic failure, diagnostic difficulties, the impact of work on their family life, and the death of young patients.

The argument continues between those who believe the special stress theory and those who favour an explanation in terms of the preselection into medicine of a vulnerable minority who are especially at risk of later breakdown. Sick doctors themselves almost invariably explain their illness in terms of overwhelming pressure of work, as do their professional representatives (Sellers, 1978), but objective research has repeatedly failed to confirm this (Waring, 1977).

The Contribution of Specific Conditions to Doctors' Increased Morbidity

Only once we have acknowledged the general excess of psychiatric morbidity among doctors can we consider the contribution of specific disorders such as alcoholism. Murray (1977) found that overall psychiatric hospitalisation rates for Scottish male doctors were among more than twice those of Social Class 1 controls, but this difference was not evenly-spread throughout the different diagnostic categories. There were no significant differences in the rates for schizophrenia, dementia, personality disorder and neurosis, but drug dependence, alcoholism and depression were all significantly more common among doctors, with the greatest disparities being in drug dependence and alcoholism.

All studies of mentally-ill doctors have emphasised the frequency of depression (Table 4.1). The frequency of suicide by doctors also attests, by implication, to a high prevalence of depression; as can be seen in Table 4.2 the Registrar General's reports on occupational mortality in England and Wales have consistently shown that doctors are especially likely to take their own lives. Other health care workers such as pharmacists and nurses appear to share doctors' predeliction for suicide (Table 4.3). Possible reasons for this are (a) their contact with disease and death, and (b) their access to drugs.

Table 4.2: Standard Mortality Ratios from Suicide and Cirrhosis among Doctors (England and Wales, 1921—71)

	1921	1931	1951	1961	1971
Suicide	201	109	226	176	335
Cirrhosis	185	183	250	350	311

Source: Office of Population Censuses and Surveys.

Table 4.3: Occupational Groups with a High Mortality from Suicide (England and Wales, 1970—2)

Occupation	SMR
Pharmacists	464
Chiropodists	374
Labourers	370
Medical practitioners	335
Housekeepers	321
Medical workers	320
Bricklayers	313
Nurses	297

Source: Office of Population Censuses and Surveys.

Many investigators have pointed out that drug dependence appears to be an occupational hazard for doctors (Modlin and Montes, 1977; Green, Carroll and Buxton, 1976) and blamed the causal combination of a predisposing personality with the ready availability of drugs. It is less easy to understand why doctors should be especially prone to alcoholism. But evidence (Murray, 1977) has shown that annual hospital discharge rates for alcoholism in Scotland were 3.3 times greater for doctors than for controls. The excess was particularly marked in middle age (Figure 4.2); indeed, 58 per cent of hospitalisations of male doctors between the ages of 45 and 54 years were attributable to alcoholism.

These findings accord with the widespread assumption that doctors are especially prone to alcoholism, and the evidence from the other series of mentally-ill doctors previously described (Table 4.1). In addition, Simon and Lumly (1968) found that 25 of their 36 hospitalised physician-patients were alcoholic; while Sclare (1978a) reported that 30 of the 100 sick doctors he studied were alcoholic, and Glatt (1974) noted that over a 25-year period the proportion of doctors among alcoholics admitted to two English specialised units was two to four per cent. Glatt (1978) has estimated the number of alcoholic doctors in Britain as being 'in the region of 2,000 to 3,000', while Bissell and Jones (1976) consider that in the USA between 13,600 and 22,600 doctors are or will become alcoholics. These figures are, of course, no more than intelligent guesses.

Additional evidence of the frequency of alcoholism in the profession comes from the Registrar General's data regarding deaths from liver cirrhosis among doctors in England and Wales over the past 50 years. These have consistently shown (Table 4.2) an excess of such deaths among doctors. It is, of course, possible that cirrhosis in doctors may be related to different aetiological factors than in the general population. Certainly health care personnel are more at risk of hepatitis B infection (Denes *et al.*, 1978) particularly if they work in renal dialysis units (Druckker, Schoutten and Alberts, 1968), and there has been one unconfirmed suggestion that hepatitis B infection may predispose to the development of alcoholic cirrhosis (Druckker *et al.*, 1972). However, if exposure to hepatitis B were the crucial factor then nurses who share doctors' increased exposure ought to have a similarly high death rate from cirrhosis — in fact their SMR is below that of the general population!

Figure 4.2: Discharge Rates for Alcoholism from Scottish Psychiatric Inpatient Beds of Male Doctors and Social Class 1 Controls

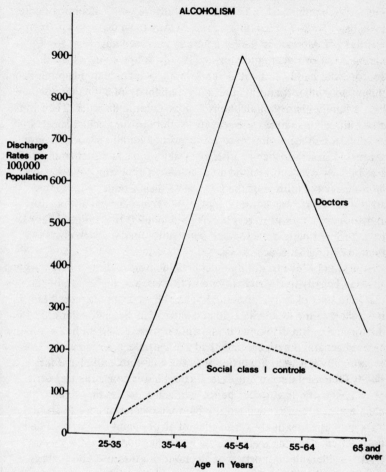

The Characteristics of Alcoholic Doctors

Two studies published in 1976 dealt specifically with alcoholic doctors. Bissell and Jones (1976) interviewed 98 American doctors who were members of Alcoholics Anonymous and had been abstinent for a minimum of one year, and Murray (1976b) followed-up 41 alcoholic doctors who had been treated at a London postgraduate hospital. From these two studies it appears that only a minority of alcoholic doctors have a family history of alcoholism or psychiatric disorder. Their pre-alcoholic careers range from repeated failure to spectacular success. Among British alcoholic doctors a surprisingly high proportion have graduated from Scottish or Irish medical schools, and such graduates are similarly over-represented among doctors appearing before the disciplinary committee of the General Medical Council on charges arising out of alcohol abuse. Cargill (1976) calculated that Scottish and Irish graduates were respectively 5.5 and 9.0 times more likely to be brought before the General Medical Council on such charges than their English counterparts.

Murray (1976b) found that alcoholic doctors had most often begun to drink heavily in their twenties and thirties, and the length of time from the start of heavy drinking to alcoholism being diagnosed ranged from six months to 25 years. In one particular case a 42-year-old doctor had begun drinking during army service and when he entered general practice usually had a few drinks after work. He occasionally got tight at parties or at the golf club, and his intake slowly increased until by his late thirties he was consuming a bottle of whisky daily. In the year before admission he was intoxicated most evenings and needed a drink before morning surgery to steady his hands. His breath always smelled of alcohol and the patients had noticed him swigging from a bottle between house-calls.

A considerable proportion of alcoholic doctors also abuse drugs; some begin drinking in the wake of well-established drug dependence, but more commonly the hung-over doctor begins to experiment with other drugs and becomes dependent on them too.

Alcoholism may occasionally arise in the context of a psychiatric illness such as anxiety neurosis, depression or personality disorder (Sclare, 1978a). However all too frequently those whom the drinking doctor eventually consults refuse to deal with the alcoholism itself and regard it merely as a symptom of an underlying disorder. Bissell and Jones (1976) found that 34 of their 98 alcoholic doctors had discussed the question of alcoholism with a therapist only to have the latter dismiss the possibility.

Consequences of Alcoholism

Alcoholic doctors accumulate many of the same sequelae of their addiction as alcoholics without medical qualifications. Upper alimentary tract disorder, delirium tremens, marital breakdown, and drunken-driving offences are especially common. Suicide is a particular risk because it is difficult for a doctor to take an overdose as a 'cry for help' and retain his dignity. Because of his knowledge of the lethal dose of drugs a suicidal gesture is immediately seen for what it is. One of the author's doctor-patients stated that he had taken an overdose 'to make my wife more sympathetic. It didn't work – she just laughed at me.'

Although police are reluctant to apprehend a doctor, Bissell and Jones (1976) reported that their 98 physicians had accumulated a total of 219 arrests and 170 jailings. A doctor's physical symptoms and outrageous social behaviour are particularly often wrongly-attributed to organic disease with resultant unnecessary investigation and delay in diagnosis.

There are further hazards for the alcoholic doctor. Forging prescriptions for psychotropic medications can insidiously become a habit, formerly distinguished careers are damaged and patient care is invariably affected. Strega (1978) has graphically described the horrifying progress of an alcoholic surgeon:

> It was generally accepted that on those Monday mornings when he did not have 'flu' he would be irrational and erratic to an extreme. One of his fads was to make a firm, definite, but totally inaccurate diagnosis and demand immediate action be taken upon it.

The hospital staff responded to these commands to assist at hazardous operations by a variety of delaying subterfuges including temporarily losing the patient at risk and removing the operating theatre lights. Unfortunately, they were unable to prevent the unnecessary death of one patient.

Surprisingly patients are very tolerant of their doctors' alcoholic indiscretions. Butcher (1978) believes that this is because they can identify with a doctor who is 'an ordinary weak mortal like themselves', particularly if his weakness is towards women or drinking.

However, a minority of alcoholic doctors find themselves before their professional disciplinary board. Of 97 doctors whose cases were considered by the British General Medical Council in 1974 but not referred further, 39 resulted from the abuse of alcohol; 14 of the more serious cases considered by the Disciplinary Committee of the same body also arose from alcohol abuse (General Medical Council, 1974). In the USA, disciplinary action for alcoholism was taken against 3.2 per cent of those licensed in Arizona during an eleven-year period, but against only one per cent of those licensed in Connecticut over six years (AMA Council on Mental Health, 1973).

Interspeciality Differences

There have been suggestions that a doctor's speciality may affect his likelihood of mental illness in general and alcoholism in particular. For instance, a'Brook and his colleagues (1967) claimed that psychiatrists were over-represented among their sick doctors. Subsequently, Waring (1974) administered the General Health Questionnaire to 83 English psychiatric trainees and 35 medical postgraduates; 22 per cent of the psychiatric trainees had a score 'in the range of a probable case of non-psychotic illness' compared with only three per cent of non-psychiatric trainees. However, Waring (1975) failed to replicate this difference among Canadian post-graduates, and Toone *et al.* (1980) found junior psychiatrists to have similar neuroticism scores to controls, on the Eysenck Personality Questionnaire. Blacky and Rosow (1973) claimed that psychiatrists had a higher risk of suicide than any other subspeciality, but this has not been confirmed (Rose and Rosow, 1973).

Similar arguments rage in relation to alcoholism. Bissell and Jones (1976) noted that 'a striking proportion of the alcoholic physicians identified themselves as psychiatrists'. In contrast, Murray (1976b) found that only six per cent of the psychiatrists referred to the Maudsley Hospital were diagnosed as alcoholic, compared with 33 per cent of surgeons and 37 per cent of general practitioners. Franklin (1977) and Sclare (1978a) have also examined this question of specialty, and both concluded that it is general practitioners who have the highest risk of alcoholism. Such disparities between the different reports are most likely a reflection of the unrepresentative nature of the samples studied.

Referral and Treatment

Edwards (1975) has written perceptively of the way in which doctors only too often fail to help their alcoholic colleagues:

> For the doctor alcoholic, the familiar history is therefore of a period of very dangerous drinking during which his colleagues have turned a blind eye, with the story developing to a crisis which is met with misunderstanding and rejection. This biphasic course is predictable.

Illustrations of connivance with dangerously alcoholic doctors are many. Strega (1978) has recently described the instance of an eminent surgeon:

> . . . the extent of his drinking was acknowledged throughout the hospital. The subject was rarely discussed openly and then only with a mixture of jocularity ('Guess what he did next?') and hopelessness ('Well how could I stop him?') Nothing it seemed could threaten his inviolability, supported as he was by a pyramid of housemen, registrars, lecturers, and research fellows. If one man had stepped out of line the whole fragile construction would have fallen; but whether out of loyalty to the gifted surgeon he once was or whether out of fear for the power of a referee, nobody moved a muscle.

Alcoholic doctors only rarely seek help entirely of their own accord, and even then they are concerned not so much with their alcohol consumption as with the adverse consequences of that consumption. Most are pushed forward very late in the course of their illness by long-suffering wives, disappointed colleagues or alarmed employers. Many of these have refrained from expressing private concern or have covered up for prolonged periods only to have to act precipitously because of an unavoidable crisis. Other sick doctors come to light by chance. For example, a 50-year-old doctor developed a tremor after a routine operation and on the third day claimed that he was surrounded by threatening figures who had electrified his bed. He became delirious, had a convulsion, and was subsequently discovered to have been drinking nearly a bottle of vodka daily for several years.

Once the alcoholic doctor is referred to a psychiatrist his care is essentially that of any alcoholic. This is more difficult than it sounds since, as Edwards (1975) states, 'the temptation at this stage is for each actor to be telephoning all other parties at dead of night, giving information which is of no account to be passed on, and trying to set up a series of secret contacts'. Furthermore, some doctors find it difficult to adopt the patient-role, and their psychiatrists frequently find it impossible to adhere to the consistent therapeutic policies that they apply to other patients.

For alcoholics in general there is little evidence that inpatient treatment is superior to outpatient care. However, in the case of the alcoholic doctor, admission prevents the doctor practising or rather malpractising; it therefore protects the public against a potentially-dangerous practitioner, and protects the doctor against the possible consequences of his misjudgements when under the influence. In most cases, therefore, the alcoholic doctor should be admitted to hospital under the care of a psychiatrist with specialised knowledge of alcoholism. This may on occasion involve hospitalisation some distance from home, but this is not necessarily a disadvantage since it may prevent the precise nature of the illness becoming public knowledge among the doctor's colleagues and patients. All alcoholic doctors should at least be introduced to AA. Not all will find it useful, but for those who do there is a section of AA for alcoholic doctors.

Following hospitalisation, which may last for anything from a few weeks to several months, therapy should be continued on a long-term supportive basis. The question will inevitably arise as to whether or not the patient-doctor should return to clinical practice. Any doctor who is drinking should be very strongly advised against working with patients since he runs the risk of destroying both his patients' health and his own career. Some experienced psychiatrists insist on their doctor-alcoholics avoiding patient care until they have been sober for at least six months.

Outcome

Murray (1976b) followed-up 36 alcoholic doctors for a mean period of 63 months. Four almost certainly killed themselves, one died from cirrhosis, and two died of causes unconnected with their alcoholism. Of the total 36, only seven completely overcame their drinking problem, and ten had less than one relapse per year. But ten suffered more than one relapse per year and nine continued almost constant dependent-drinking. Of the 29 doctors alive at follow-up, only eight were practising satisfactorily and a further six with varying degrees of incompetence.

The high risk of suicide is hardly surprising since the suicide rate of all hospitalised alcoholics is about 25 times that of the general population. Indeed, alcoholism may be a major contributory factor to the high suicide rate generally recorded for doctors (Edwards, 1975). Blacky and Rosow (1973) studied 80 doctors who killed themselves and found that 39 per cent were described as alcoholic, while Simon and Lumry (1968) reported that 25 of their 36 suicidal physicians were alcoholic.

Murray, from his 1976b study, concluded that it is disappointing that so many potentially-able doctors were unable to overcome their addiction and return to practising good medicine. But the study may have been biased towards such a finding by the fact that two-thirds of the subjects had previosuly undergone psychiatric treatment and had failed to achieve a lasting recovery. Both Glatt (1974) and Bissell and Jones (1976) believe that the prognosis is much less bleak. Certainly the fact that Bissell and Jones (1976) were able to collect 98 abstinent doctors attests to the existence of many who do overcome alcoholism.

Conclusion

The reader of this book will, probably, by now accept the premise that occupation is an important predisposing factor to alcoholism. But, in contrast to other occupations where the causes are relatively clear, the reasons for the medical profession's increased liability to harmful drinking are poorly understood. In further contrast to other occupations where alcoholism can often be seen as an isolated liability, alcohol abuse by doctors is best regarded as one manifestation of a general proneness to psychiatric disorder and to dependence and depression in particular. Medicine may preferentially attract a minority of students who are especially vulnerable to later breakdown, and there is some partially-convincing evidence that the practice of clinical medicine may be particularly anxiety-provoking. These factors go some way towards explaining the increased overall rates for admission to mental hospitals found among doctors, but do not account for the even higher rates for alcoholism.

Until recently medical students were overwhelmingly male. As medical training is considerably longer than most other professional courses this meant that potential doctors spent a longer period in a predominantly male student group. The implications of prolonged exposure to such groups have been described elsewhere in this volume. An ability to hold one's liquor is said to be almost mandatory for medical students. The majority of them enjoy trying to measure up to this caricature, but for an unfortunate few heavy-drinking as undergraduates or junior doctors may be the prelude to later alcoholism. Ready access to drugs may predispose doctors not only to drug dependence but also to switch to alcohol abuse if suspected of over-prescribing for themselves. Some doctors may discover during the course of other psychiatric disorders, such as depression or anxiety neurosis, that alcohol relieves their suffering. Then once heavy-drinking patterns are established they may be reinforced by the relatively affluent social and economic milieu in which doctors live and work.

5 ALCOHOL PROBLEMS AND THE FISHING INDUSTRY IN NORTH-EAST SCOTLAND

Keith J.B. Rix

In 1975 the Aberdeen and District Council on Alcoholism arranged a meeting with the local advisory committee of the Royal National Mission to Deep Sea Fishermen in order to discuss the subject of alcoholism in the fishing industry. The council arranged the meeting after realising that a number of its clients were fishermen but it was also familiar with the 'widely held impression in Aberdeen that fishermen are excessive drinkers' (Stuart *et al.*, 1967). However, the advisory committee, which included a member of the local fishing vessel owners' association, a trade union official and an official from the local industry's disciplinary committee, expressed the view that 'there was no significant drinking problem among trawler fishermen' (Scottish Council on Alcoholism, 1975).

In order to investigate this issue further a research project was initiated which sought evidence concerning the rate of alcoholism in fishermen. Three lines of enquiry were pursued. First, a literature search was made for evidence relating to the drinking habits of seafarers, and, in particular, fishermen. Secondly, official publications and public records concerning the fishing industry were studied in order to ascertain how far the government and the fishing industry had considered the possibility that the industry suffered from a high rate of alcohol-related problems. Thirdly, the psychiatric case register for the north-east of Scotland was used to ascertain the numbers of fishermen who were diagnosed as alcoholic for the first time in the years 1966 to 1970. The results of these three lines of enquiry are described in the three sections of this chapter which follow the section describing the occupation of fishing.

Having established from the case register study that there was an increased risk of fishermen being diagnosed as alcoholic compared to the rest of the male population, a search was made of the hospital records of alcoholic fishermen in the hope of learning something about the possible cause of the high incidence. The records were also used to obtain information about patterns of drinking and the types of alcohol-related problems which occur in fishermen. The fifth and sixth sections of this chapter describe the results of these two aspects of the hospital records study.

The final section contains some tentative suggestions of measures which the fishing industry might consider for reducing the prevalence and incidence of alcoholism. However, before proceeding further it is necessary to understand something of the way in which the fishing industry is organised.

The Occupation of Fishing

The idea that the term 'fisherman' means nothing is attributed to G.L. Grant who studied the morbidity of a group of Aberdeen trawlermen (Moore, 1969a). He was referring to the many kinds of fishermen ranging from the crofter fishermen of the Highlands and Islands on the one hand to the distant-water fishermen who sail from such ports as Hull, Grimsby, Fleetwood and, to a lesser extent, Aberdeen, on the other.

Broadly speaking, fishermen can be divided into two groups: inshore and deep-sea fishermen. The group of deep-sea fishermen is subdivided into three further groups according to the waters in which they fish: near-, middle-, and distant-water fishermen.

Inshore fishermen use boats which are usually less than 40 feet in length. The fish are caught in pots or with handlines and the fishermen operate singly or in crews of two or three. Catches are landed daily which means that the fishermen return home at night. The boats are, in the main, owned and operated on a share basis. The skipper and his part-owners share equally the income from each trip with other members of the crew. No one actually receives a wage. Inshore fishermen sail from the small fishing 'creeks' along the Moray Firth and Aberdeenshire coasts.

Near-water vessels do not exceed 110 feet in length and carry crews of up to twelve. Fish are caught with a seine net or by trawling. Some seine-netters sail from the smaller ports such as Peterhead, Buckie and Fraserburgh, but the trawlers sail mainly from Lowestoft, Aberdeen and Grimsby. These vessels fish in the North Sea, the English Channel, the Minch and the Western Approaches. They leave port on a Sunday night or Monday morning and trips last five or six days. This means that the fishermen are often home for the weekends. Some of the vessels are owned on a share basis, usually by the skipper, mate and engineer, but others, particularly the larger vessels, are company-owned. Fishermen employed on these company-owned vessels receive a basic daily wage supplemented by additional payments for each trip which are based on the size of the catch landed.

Middle-water vessels are between 110 and 140 feet in length and they sail mainly from Aberdeen, Grimsby and Fleetwood. They fish around the Faroes and Rockall and the continental shelf to the west and north of Scotland. Fish are caught by trawling and trips last up to two weeks. Crews number between ten and 14 men except on the larger vessels which may carry as many as 20 men.

While the near- and middle-water vessels do not experience the Arctic temperatures which plague distant-water vessels, they are subject to gales which may be just as severe as those in distant waters. In good weather these vessels may sail further afield, the near-water vessels sailing into middle waters and the middle-water vessels sailing into distant waters.

Distant-water vessels are over 140 feet in length and sail mainly from Hull, Grimsby and Fleetwood. Only a few distant-water vessels are in the Aberdeen fleet. They fish in the Barents Sea, around Bear Island and Iceland, and off the coasts of north Norway, south-west Greenland and Newfoundland. There are three types of large trawler. The older vessels which haul the trawl over the side of the boat are called side or side-winding trawlers. Newer stern trawlers haul the trawl over the stern. The crews of these vessels number between twelve and 20. The third type is a large stern trawler which freezes the catch on board instead of storing it on ice. It is called a freezer trawler. Between 20 and 30 men are carried on freezer trawlers. These distant-water vessels make trips which may last more than three weeks.

Most fishermen are employed on a casual basis and at the end of a trip the company is under no obligation to allow a fisherman to sign on for the next voyage. Further insecurity arises out of the fact that the wages vary with the amount of fish landed.

In the mid 1960s there were almost 10,000 fishermen in Scotland (excluding crofter fishermen) and two-thirds of these were in north-east Scotland, Orkney and Shetland, which is the area containing Scotland's largest fishing port and the third largest fishing port in the United Kingdom, Aberdeen. In 1965 the Aberdeen fleet comprised 50 near-water, 62 middle-water and two distant-water vessels.

By comparing the duration of the fishing trips and the range of environmental conditions experienced by the different types of vessel, it is apparent that there is a range of occupational experience within the group of men designated 'fishermen'. Apart from employment and monetary differences, or perhaps to some extent as a result of them,the inshore and some of the near-water fishermen differ both culturally and socially from most deep-sea fishermen. The former are more likely to be influenced by the social and religious mores of life in the fishing villages and small towns with their closely-knit families. Deep-sea fishermen from cities like Aberdeen come under different influences. It seems reasonable to suggest that some of the factors which distinguish the lifestyles of the different fishermen are ones which will also influence their drinking patterns. Although there is no empirical evidence to substantiate this view there is much anecdotal evidence which suggests that there is a great variability of drinking habits within the fishing industry.

Although crofter fishermen were excluded from the hospital records study of alcoholic fishermen, the records study otherwise covers the range of fishermen — from inshore to distant-water, from men from small fishing creeks such as Rosehearty and Inverallochy to men from the small ports of Fraserburgh and Peterhead and the large port of Aberdeen. However, the medical and sociological literature on the occupation of fishing is weighted considerably towards the deep-sea fisherman and if this chapter appears to focus on aspects of the deep-sea fisherman's work it must not be taken to imply that it is only deep-sea fishermen who are at risk of alcoholism.

Drinking and the Sea

Much more fascinating than a search of the medical and scientific literature is a study of sea shanties and folk songs which contain ample testimony to the part which alcohol plays in the life of the seafarer (e.g. *Row Bullies Row*[1]) and the problems which it may cause (e.g. *What Shall We Do with the Drunken Sailor?*). Other anecdotal evidence comes from a number of sources. J.B. Priestley in his *English Journey* quoted a trawler owner who described trawler crews as 'a race apart, perhaps the last of the wild men in this tamed island of ours, fellows capable of working day and night without food and sleep . . . and then capable of going on the booze with equal energy and enthusiasm'. An alcoholic seaman has described alcoholism as an occupational disease of seamen (J.I.F., 1947).

While medical and scientific research has confirmed the existence of heavy drinking and alcoholism in seafaring populations, the evidence for seafarers being at increased risk of alcoholism is not very great. About one-fifth of men passing through Merchant Marine 'rest centers' in the United States at the end of the Second World War were described as having 'alcohol addiction' (Heath, 1945; Powdermaker, 1945) but these were self-selected groups of men unlikely to be representative of all merchant seamen. In a group of 100 British merchant-navy officers and crew 26 per cent were found to be 'heavy drinkers' and 25 per cent 'very heavy drinkers' (Rose and Glatt, 1961). However, the authors did not indicate what percentage were alcoholic and there was no control group. Another uncontrolled study of 3,447 Norwegian merchant seamen found that 14 per cent were 'alcohol abusers' (Brun-Gulbrandsen and Irgen-Jensen, 1967). The over-representation of seamen in Swedish clinic, institution and temperance board series of alcoholics (Amark, 1951) does not necessarily indicate an increased rate of alcoholism in seamen. A study of the incidence of psychosis in various occupational groups in Norway, based on hospital admission data, found that the incidence of alcoholic psychosis in merchant seamen (officers excluded) was second only to the incidence in salesmen and waiters while the officers had very low rates (Ødegaard, 1956). Incidence rates for alcoholism have also been calculated for enlisted men in the United States Navy and Marine Corps (Gunderson and Schuckit, 1975) and for Navy and Marine Corps officers (Schuckit and Gunderson, 1974a). However, their comparison of the rates with those reported by Walsh (1969) for male civilian populations in the United Kingdom is unsatisfactory for a number of reasons.

Evidence of a different kind is that found in liver cirrhosis mortality statistics (see Table 2.1). These indicate that seamen are six or seven times as likely to die of liver cirrhosis as the general population.

In contrast to the numerous studies on drinking in merchant seamen and the US Navy, there are few such studies concerning the fishing industry. The study of the incidence of psychoses in various occupational groups in Norway showed a negligible incidence of alcoholic psychosis in fishermen but this result was regarded as an artefact because the majority of Norwegian fishermen live in northern Norway where all admission rates are low (Ødegaard, 1956). However, there is evidence suggestive of an increased risk of alcoholism in British fishermen. The liver cirrhosis mortality statistics (Table 2.1) point to an increased risk of alcohol-related morbidity since the fishermen have six times the risk of dying of liver cirrhosis as the total male population. Blaxter (1979) has studied problem drinking in the Shetland Islands (Table 5.1) and found that the prevalence of problem drinking in fishermen and seamen was 128 per 1,000 which

Table 5.1: Rates of Problem Drinking by Occupation (Shetland)

		Rate per 1,000 males (occupied, retired or unemployed)
1.	Professional and managerial	49
2.	Owners of small businesses	58
3.	Other non-manual workers	38
4.	Skilled manual workers	92
5.	Semi- and unskilled manual workers	73
6.	Fishermen etc	128
7.	Workers in public houses etc	180
8.	Crofters etc	47

Source: Blaxter (1979). This study was conducted in 1978. Dates shown above are based on 1971 Census data. The fishermen's rate is probably higher than shown here.

was a rate over two and one half times that of crofters, over one and one half times that of semi- and unskilled manual workers, and second only to members of the alcohol trade in her eight occupational groups.

Official Findings on Drinking and the Fishing Industry

The drinking habits of fishermen have received the most attention from the industry and government in questions of trawler safety (Board of Trade, 1969) and discipline (Department of Trade, 1975).

The Holland-Martin Report of the Committee of Inquiry into Trawler Safety (Board of Trade, 1969) received a considerable amount of evidence that drinking by crews of fishing vessels is a major factor affecting trawler safety. It heard that drinking was particularly prevalent on the first day out of port 'with the result that fire and boat drills, though logged, may not be carried out'. Their concern receives some support from the observation by Richardson (1979) that there is a relationship between drinking before boarding side-winding trawlers and the injury rate in trawlermen on these vessels in the first 24 hours (Figure 5.1). Not only injuries but also fatalities may occur. A study of fatal accidents in Norwegian seamen suggested that at least one-third were associated with alcohol (Arner, 1973). Unfortunately the strength of the association between drinking and accidents at sea is likely to be obscured. A study of fatalities on Swedish ships revealed that alcohol was astoundingly common as a hidden factor and it has been commented that, for example, the official verdict is 'death by

Figure 5.1: Incidence of Accidents on Hull Side Trawlers During 1973 According to Day of Trip

☐   FIRST AID INJURIES, PERIOD OF INCAPACITY LESS THAN 24 hours.

■   PERIOD OF INCAPACITY MORE THAN 24 hours.

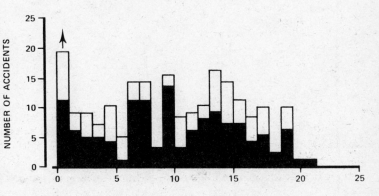

DAYS OUT OF PORT (UP TO 2359 HOURS)

Note
The arrow indicates that the number of accidents on the first day of the trip should be doubled for comparison with the other days of the trip. The reason is that since Hull is a tidal port with vessels leaving throughout the 24-hour period and since accidents are recorded as up to 2359 hours on the first day of the trip, the first column of the histogram represents accidents occurring during a mean period of only 12 hours.
Source: Richardson (1979).

drowning' when drunken seamen try to jump on or off the ship instead of using the gangway (Graz, 1973). Similar situations may arise in the fishing industry. Cadenhead (1976) has described how 'the trawlers often tie up side by side, and it is a perilous enough journey for a sober man, especially in the dark, to move from bulwark to bulwark and over hatches and fish boxes slimy with salt water and fish offal. It is easily understood, therefore, how the inebriated person comes to grief.'

The importance of more clearly establishing the role of alcohol in fishing industry accidents is underlined by the high risk of fatal accidents in fishermen which, unlike that of other industries, is not declining (Figure 5.2). The risk of fatal accidents in England and Wales fishermen is 17 times that of the male population and the risk for Scottish fishermen is nearly seven times that of the male

Figure 5.2: Fatal Accidents in Fishing, Mining and Manufacturing Industries

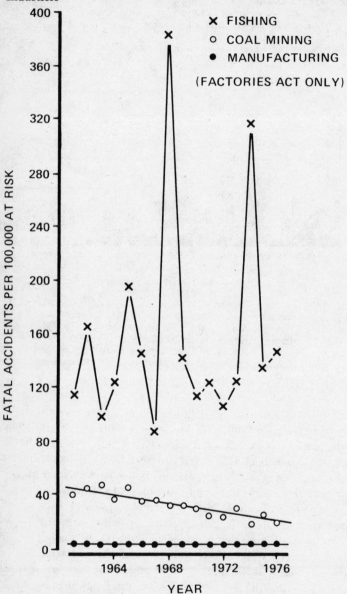

Source: Department of Community and Occupational Medicine, University of Dundee.

population (Schilling, Walford and Wood, 1969).

Official inquiries into accidents at sea are also a source of information concerning the part which alcohol plays in the life of the fisherman. The findings of the Department of Trade inquiry into the loss
of the *Wyre Victory* (Report of Court No S499) will be described
later. The collision between the *Leswood* and the *Adastra* was not
the subject of a formal Department of Trade inquiry but it resulted in
legal proceedings being taken against crew members in the Sheriff
Court of Grampian, Highland and Islands. The collision had occurred
in broad daylight when the sea was calm and visibility perfect and
Sheriff Muir Russell, before whom the case was heard, stated that in
his opinion drink appeared to be the one and only reason for the
collision. The evidence for this opinion is contained in his Stated
Case to the High Court of Justiciary in Edinburgh:

> Five cans of beer per person had been issued by the Master Walker
> between 10.30 a.m. when the vessel left harbour and 1.25 p.m.
> when Foreman, MacBeth and Neave went on watch. One can was
> issued on leaving harbour, two more were issued three-quarters
> of an hour later and two more cans at 1.25 p.m. just immediately
> before the said three men went on watch. Between leaving harbour
> and the time of the accident Foreman consumed a considerable
> amount of drink. The issue of beer was supplemented by whisky of
> his own. No check was kept on board the vessel as to how many
> cans of beer any particular man drinks and it was possible for one
> man to consume more cans if another man took less than his
> ration.
>
> By 1.25 p.m. Foreman had a 'drink in him' but his capacity was
> not impaired. His condition became worse as the watch continued;
> about 2.30 p.m. his speech was slurred and his ability to control
> the ship was impaired. Foreman and MacBeth had a bottle of whisky
> on the bridge and drank from it from time to time . . . Before the
> time of the collision, Foreman was considerably affected by alcohol
> and he was under the influence of drink to such an extent that his
> capacity to carry out his duties was impaired. His eyes were affected
> by drink, his speech was slurred and his movements were sluggish.
> He was at the wheel at the time of the collision with the *Adastra*
> and the only reason for the collision was the effect of alcohol on
> Foreman. Immediately after the impact MacBeth pushed Foreman
> away from the wheel wresting it out of his hold and took the
> wheel over himself. Whilst MacBeth had also taken a fair quantity

to drink, his tolerance to alcohol was greater and it was not established that his capacity to carry out his duties was impaired.

After the collision (at about 3 p.m.) Foreman never reported it to Walker nor even to the Mate. He just stood for a while and then sat down on a seat on the bridge and said he wanted to be put ashore. By 4.30 p.m. Foreman was still technically in charge of the watch and by that time he was even more drunk . . . Foreman was a member of the crew and the person for the time being in charge of the vessel at the time of the collision and whilst under the influence of drink he omitted to keep a proper look out or to alter course to avoid the *Adastra*; which matters were normally required for the purpose of preserving his own ship from serious damage.

There was no loss of life in the collision between the *Leswood* and the *Adastra*. This was not so in the case of the collision between the Aberdeen vessels *Ben Tarbert* and *Venturer* which collided in calm seas and good visibility outside Peterhead harbour on 28 November 1975. The *Ben Tarbert* sank within a few minutes of the collision and two of her crew were drowned. The collision appears to have resulted from the failure of the *Venturer*'s second engineer in the engine room to obey an instruction from the bridge to change course. After the collision the second engineer was found in the engine room sitting on a locker looking like 'a man in a daze'. While there was conflicting evidence about whether or not the second engineer had been drinking on his way from Buckie to join the vessel in Aberdeen, the chief engineer considered that he 'had a dram in him' when they put to sea, but he did not consider him unfit to carry out his duties. The second engineer was later found guilty of culpable homicide at Banff Sheriff Court and in the Court of Session in Edinburgh the owners of the *Ben Tarbert* were awarded £100,000 damages because the judge found that:

> The system (operated by the owners of the *Venturer*), in so far as it was designed to ensure that their employees were at all times in a fit state to carry out their duties at sea, was deficient in certain respects . . . These were matters which the defenders were not entitled to leave to the unfettered discretion of their skippers.

The Report of the Working Group on Discipline in the Fishing Industry (Department of Trade, 1975) devoted a whole chapter to 'the problem of drink' and stated that drinking played a major part in offences such as missing the ship, refusing to sail and refusing duty. The same working group also expressed a view on the prevalence of alcoholism in fishermen: 'We were told that there was little to show that alcoholism, as such, was significantly more prevalent in the fishing industry than in the population at large' and 'not more than about 15 per cent of fishermen were immoderate drinkers'.

Alcoholism in North-east Scotland Fishermen

Using the psychiatric case register for the north-east of Scotland it has been possible to establish the numbers of fishermen who received a first diagnosis of alcoholism or alcoholic psychosis in the years 1966 to 1970. The numbers of fishermen employed in the region were found in the Scottish Sea Fisheries Statistical Tables. From the two sets of figures it has been possible to calculate the incidence rates for alcoholism and alcoholic psychosis in the fishermen at risk. These have been compared with the rates for the rest of the male population. The details of this study are described elsewhere (Rix, Hunter and Olley, in preparation) and only the main results are given here.

On average, over the years 1966 to 1970, the fishermen appear to have been twice as likely to receive a diagnosis of alcoholism or alcoholic psychosis as the rest of the male population. Calculation of age-specific rates suggests that younger fishermen were particularly at risk. Those aged 20 to 29 years had incidence rates which appeared to be four times those of 20 to 29-year-old non-fishermen. Although it is possible that these increased rates reflect simply an increased rate in Social Class 4 to which fishermen belong, the results nevertheless indicate that north-east Scotland fishermen were more likely than the average male in that area to be diagnosed for the first time as suffering from alcoholism in the years 1966 to 1970.

The Origins of Alcoholism in Fishermen

Schuckit and Gunderson (1974b) have listed three factors which might explain the link between occupation and high risk of alcoholism: (a) a job milieu that promotes heavy drinking, (b) pre-existing selection factors that predispose the incipient alcoholic toward a specific occupation, and (c) factors influencing both job selection and the development of alcoholism (e.g. having a father who is alcoholic and a member of a high-risk occupation to which the son is attracted). There is a fourth factor which is a corollary of the first: a job milieu that discourages moderate drinkers with the result that the industry loses moderate drinkers and has to recruit from a residue of less-moderate drinkers. These factors can be expanded to incorporate risk factors suggested by other authors and they can be illustrated both from the general literature on fishing and seafaring and from the hospital records of alcoholic fishermen. The latter were obtained for each fisherman who first received a psychiatric diagnosis of alcoholism or alcoholic psychosis in north-east Scotland in the years 1966 to 1970.

A Job Milieu that Promotes Heavy Drinking

The *availability of alcohol* on board ship varies from one fishing vessel to another according to both official and unofficial factors. Customs regulations do not permit a bonded alcohol supply to be carried if the vessel is not sailing north of Latitude 61° North and when a bond is carried the seal may not be broken until the vessel is beyond the three-mile limit. Unofficial agreements have determined that all Lowestoft trawlers are 'dry' and many inshore vessels sailing from the small fishing creeks on the coast of the Moray Firth are owned and crewed by families who do not allow alcohol aboard. However, the Department of Trade Working Group on Discipline (1975) expressed concern that in spite of regulations there is a 'prevalent and increasing practice of holding parties (known as "cheer" parties) on board prior to and after sailing'. Such parties result not simply from breaking into the bond. Some fishermen smuggle alcohol aboard in their personal belongings but 'the principal source is bulk supplies brought to the vessel in cars or taxis by individuals or groups of men' (Department of Trade, 1975). It is hardly surprising that a 21-year-old fisherman's hospital records described him as doing 'nothing but drink the first two days at sea'.

Both availability of alcohol and *social pressure* to drink it are illustrated by a fisherman's statement that 'alcohol is nowadays not only readily available but almost obligatory aboard ship'. The pressure on young recuits has been described by Tunstall (1962):

> . . . when a young recruit strains to adjust himself to the manly behaviour of the adult fishermen he is acutely aware that a sign of successful integration with them is an ability to drink . . . Most fishing recruits probably do their first serious drinking actually on trawlers. A lad of fifteen will take a dram of whisky or rum and knock it back in one gulp, making a fierce grimace to hide the tears.

Collusion by colleagues is best illustrated by the fisherman who said that he had continued to work 'only because a companion carries him aboard drunk'. Not only do colleagues collude, but owners and officers may have *permissive attitudes* towards the use of alcohol. A doctor wrote in the records of one patient that he 'has latterly worked for a boat whose skipper is known to us as a chronic alcoholic and he described how most of the crew would be drunk on leaving the port and that they may have to lower the anchor in the fishing grounds for 24–36 hours before they could start fishing while they sobered up'. At a Department of Trade inquiry (Report of Court No S499) into the loss of the Fleetwood trawler *Wyre Victory* in the Western Isles it was concluded that the owners were largely to blame for the loss of the ship because they had turned a blind eye to the taking of illicit alcohol in their ships. Even when the owners do not turn a blind eye the Department of Trade Working Group on Discipline (1975) suggested that the practice at some ports of employing retired fishermen as watchmen to look after fishing vessels when the crew is not on board adds to the ease of smuggling aboard unauthorised supplies.

Separation from normal social or sexual relationships and *boredom* have been described by Moore (1969a) in his study of Grimsby deepsea fishermen:

> The shore worker returns home after a day's work. The fisherman remains on the job even when off duty. There is no recreation and few books on board. There is no cinema, 'local', family or friends to break up the monotony. No mail arrives. When he tires of the company of his ship-mates, there is nowhere to retire.

The *'strains and stresses'* of the fishing industry are both psychological and physical. The high mortality rate of fishermen (see Figure 5.2) must be a worry to many fishermen and the Department of Trade Working Group on Discipline (1975) has recognised that some fishermen are 'psychologically incapable of facing the prospects of a new trip without first dulling their senses by over-indulgence in alcohol'. Some of the physical discomforts have been enumerated by Moore (1969a): living conditions are cramped; continuous noise and vibration reach all parts of the vessel; and it is in continuous motion, pitching, rolling and lurching. Staying on board in such circumstances is made no easier by virtue of the fact that the deck may be slippery with sea water and fish offal. Moore (1969a) has also referred to the more extreme problems of the distant water fishermen: the weather may be severe with 'freezing temperatures, when the deck and rigging of trawlers may be coated with tons of ice, and gales lasting days on end add to the trawlerman's difficulties. For the six winter months of the year, fishing takes place in continuous darkness.' Tunstall (1962) has described the fatigue: 'The job is extreme in the number of hours worked; at the fishing grounds, deckhands can be on duty for 180 hours in ten days of active fishing; deck learners, who may be no more than 16 years old, nevertheless also do 18 hours work a day for ten days in succession.' He also quoted a fisherman who said: 'Of course fishermen get drunk. Anybody who does what we do has to get drunk to stay sane.'

It has been suggested that *insecurity* is another feature of an occupation which may predispose to heavy drinking. At the time of writing, fishermen do not have contracts with specific companies and although they are likely to be allowed to sign on for the next trip at 'settling time', this is not guaranteed. Although they receive a standard basic wage, a supplement is paid which is proportional to the amount of fish landed. Thus, they have security of neither earnings nor employment.

Pre-existing Selection Factors

Schilling (1966) has described fishermen as 'a self-selected group of very unusual men' and the Board of Trade (1969) has recognised that 'deep-sea fishing attracts very unusual men who follow an arduous and exacting job'. Similar views have been expressed concerning seamen in general. Sundby (1956), who found a high rate of psychotic illness in Norwegian seamen, referred to the 'recruiting of unsuitable men', but his conclusion is not fully justified since his comparison was with other psychotic patients. Ødegaard (1956) also studied Norwegian seamen and attributed their high admission rates for schizophrenia and psychoses with epilepsy and mental deficiency to 'unfavourable selection rather than environmental factors'. He suggested that 'certain mentally-unstable persons are positively attracted to sea life, or they resort to the sea after having failed in other occupations'. Although he found in the same study that fishermen had a very low admission rate for psychoses, he attributed this to their living in an area of Norway where all admission rates for psychosis were low. Rose and Glatt (1961) found evidence of psychopathic personality disorder in 21 out of 100 British merchant seamen and even in the absence of control group data this appears to be an unusually high prevalence of psychopathy.

Examination of the hospital records of the 76 north-east Scotland fishermen revealed that personality disorder had been diagnosed in 23 and in 15 of these cases it was psychopathic personality disorder. There was a history of alcoholism in the first degree relatives of 32 out of the 76 fishermen and a further eight had parents who were totally opposed to the use of alcohol. These observations that over a half had a personality disorder or a family history of alcoholism or both is consistent with the operation of *pre-selection of personalities at risk of alcoholism*, but it is not conclusive evidence since there is no evidence to suggest that the fishing industry attracts excessive numbers of such men.

At least six men had been discharged from the navy or armed forces for offences of drunkenness which suggests a *failure to check references* of men entering the industry for the first time. Further evidence suggests that there is a failure to check references when men move within the industry. At least 17 men had been convicted of offences related to indiscipline at port or at sea, had been suspended from port registers or banned from sailing. Nevertheless they still managed to go to sea. One fisherman who had been suspended for being drunk on board ship said that this usually meant that he would be back at sea in six months. Another had been banned from sailing in Aberdeen but managed to sail from other ports. A third had lost several ships but was able to continue in the industry because the small boats in Lerwick do not operate a register.

At least 30 men had been *previously in seafaring or other 'high-risk' occupations* such as the drink trade. However, the decision to change from being a merchant seaman to being a fisherman may have much more to do with a love of the sea and relevant occupational skills than with the opportunities for excessive drinking. Therefore, it does not follow that all 30 were heavy drinkers before they entered the fishing industry, although this does appear to have been so in at least 14 whose heavy drinking began in the Merchant Navy or armed forces. Some of these had moved to other high-risk occupations before becoming fishermen. One man had been discharged from the Royal Navy as a result of his drunkenness, worked first as a barman, then as a salesman before becoming a trawler fisherman.

Factors Affecting Job Selection and the Development of Alcoholism

Six men were not only following a family tradition in selecting fishing as an occupation. They also brought to it a familial predisposition towards alcoholism.

A Job Milieu that Discourages Moderate Drinkers

It has already been suggested that the ready availability of alcohol on fishing vessels, the social pressure on fishermen to drink and permissive attitudes towards the use of alcohol on fishing vessels contribute to a job milieu which promotes heavy drinking. The existence of a heavy-drinking job milieu can have two important effects. First, it may discourage more moderate drinkers from staying in the industry. This effect was suggested in correspondence in *The Scotsman* by Ian Barclay who stated that those who use alcohol to dull the experiences of the first day or two out of port 'are an additional irritant and extra hazard and contribute nothing to brighten the experience of those who don't'. He went on to suggest that 'drunkenness on board ship does more to drive out good men than ever did poor accommodation, bad food and long voyages or hazardous operations'. Secondly, such a job milieu may discourage moderate drinkers from entering the industry with the result that the industry has to recruit from less-moderate drinkers.

Alcohol-related Problems in Fishermen

Not all fishermen drink and not all of those who do so drink to excess. But those who do drink to excess run the risk of developing alcohol-related problems. Using information obtained during the first, and in some instances the subsequent, contacts with the north-east Scotland fishermen who received a first diagnosis of alcoholism or alcoholic psychosis between 1966 and 1970, it has been possible to identify some of the alcohol-related problems which may occur in fishermen. No significance should be attached to their frequency of occurrence since this was a retrospective hospital records study and since those fishermen who received a psychiatric diagnosis of alcoholism are unlikely to be a representative sample of alcoholics in the industry.

Alcohol-related problems in fishermen can be divided into three groups: the consequences of drinking ashore, the consequences of drinking ashore followed by alcohol withdrawal at sea, and the consequences of drinking at sea.

Drinking Ashore

Eleven fishermen specifically denied drinking at sea when their case histories were obtained and the case records of four men indicated that they were regarded as good workers. For one man the records stated: 'works well at sea but spends his days on land drinking heavily and going about in drunken oblivion. A typical day ashore is spent in the pubs and drinking with friends at home between pub hours.' However, such drinking may not be without its complications. Fourteen men had been 'paid off', sacked, suspended or banned from fishing as a result of arriving drunk at the boat, refusing to sail or missing their boat. Such behaviour may delay the departure of the boat and this can be very costly for the owners. One Aberdeen company is reported as having to send taxis to collect the crew so that the boats could sail on time (Stuart *et al.*, 1967). In 1967 the company's bill for taxis came to about £1,000 *per annum* but the company lost about £250 each day a boat had to wait in port until she was fully crewed.

The behaviour of drunken fishermen in foreign ports has also given particular cause for concern because the alcohol-related problems in these circumstances are potentially political in nature. This was the view expressed in a front-page editorial comment in the *Trawling Times* of January 1975 when the behaviour of British fishermen in a Norwegian port over the festive season came:

> . . . at a time when an unusual tension was developing in our two countries over the 'no trawl' zones issue . . . Getting boozed up on board is bad enough but doing the same in another country is rapidly becoming unforgiveable at a time when the British trawlerman abroad is increasingly regarded as a representative of his country. What might at one time have been regarded as an indiscretion can easily build, these days, into a major incident.

Out of the present series of 76 fishermen at least 20 had a criminal record and at least six had been in prison. Again such behaviour is not inconsistent with a high level of work performance. One man who assaulted his wife when he was drunk, resulting in her admission to hospital, was described as 'highly thought of among the trawlers as a worker'. While it is reasonable to suspect that many of the crimes of these fishermen may have been alcohol-related, it is probable that personality disorder also played a part.

The mortality data of fishermen indicate that not only do they have an increased risk of accidents at work, but they also have an increased risk of accidents when not at work (Schilling, Walford and Wood, 1969). The present study affords an example of a non-fatal accident in a

30-year-old man who had fallen into the harbour when drunk and who had been rescued by the police. The hospital records report that the policeman received a medal and the fisherman was fined £15. It is likely that many accidents, fatal and non-fatal, are alcohol-related, and again the role of personality disorder cannot be discounted. However, the considerable importance of alcohol is suggested by the observation of Cadenhead (1976) that 'alcoholic inebriation' was associated with all of the injuries to fishermen *in port* which required emergency admission to the Gilbert Bain Hospital, Lerwick, Shetland, between 1969 and 1975. Most of these injuries were sustained as a result of falls on the way back to the ship, but some resulted from drunken brawls.

Ashore or at sea fishermen have an increased risk of suffering from illnesses which are known to be alcohol-related. They have an increased risk of peptic ulceration (Department of Health for Scotland, 1935) and although it has been suggested that this leads to fishermen seeking work on shore (Grant, 1961) there were, nevertheless, ten fishermen in the present study with a history of peptic ulceration. Such conditions are important not only in terms of the health of the individual fishermen but also in terms of the economics of the fishing industry. For example, bleeding or perforated peptic ulcer and the related condition of alcoholic gastritis may necessitate the interruption of a fishing trip in order that the affected fisherman can receive hospital treatment. Such an incident is known as a 'medical disembarkation' and can be very expensive for the trawler company. A loss of several thousand pounds may result from just two or three days lost fishing, extra fuel is needed for the journey to and from the hospital, fees for medical treatment in foreign ports can be high, and repatriation costs may be incurred if the patient is unable to travel home by trawler. The contribution of gastro-intestinal illness to medical disembarkations is shown in Table 5.2. The figures are consistent with the 22 per cent contribution of gastro-intestinal illness to the illnesses of all fishermen treated by the Royal Naval medical officers of the Fishery Protection Squadron of the Icelandic patrol in 1963 (Moore, 1969b). The precise contribution of alcohol-related gastro-intestinal illness is not known, but in view of the association of alcoholism with gastritis and peptic ulceration, the contribution is not likely to be insignificant.

Reference has already been made to the fisherman's increased risk of dying from liver cirrhosis and this may contribute to the excess mortality, apart from accidents, found in men under 45 years of age in a prospective study of 2,900 Aberdeen trawlermen (Harley and

Table 5.2: The Contribution of Gastro-intestinal Illness to Medical Disembarkations of Fishing Vessels

	Per cent of all medical disembarkations
Gilbert Bain Hospital, Shetland[1]	
January 1969–July 1975	28
Hull deep-sea fishing fleet[2]	22
Scrabster, Caithness[3]	
All gastro-intestinal illness	11
Excluding appendicitis, diarrhoea and	
vomiting, and sea sickness	5

[1] Cadenhead (1976).
[2] Richardson (1979).
[3] Mair and Deans (1979).

Backett, cited in Schilling, 1966).

Alcohol Withdrawal at Sea

One man was described as drinking excessively ashore but at sea 'he is busy and occupied and alcohol does not concern him'. Some of the other fishermen were less fortunate and at least seven had experienced alcohol withdrawal symptoms at sea. One described taking several days to improve while at sea and another described withdrawal tremulousness. A 38-year-old spent £250 and drank continuously for twelve days during which time he was continuously drunk. He worked as usual for the first four days at sea. Then, at night in his bunk, he fell under a spell. He heard the voices of his relatives taking him through the whole of his life. He heard the voice of a girl he knew telling him to hit his pal over the head with a spanner, throw him over the side and jump after him. She also told him to sit up like a dog and bark. For a 36-year-old, withdrawal hallucinations were a regular occurrence. According to his hospital records 'every time he goes to sea, he has four difficult days with aural hallucinations (bagpipes), severe shakiness and visual delusions'. When one fisherman developed withdrawal hallucinations his boat had to return to port in order that he could be compulsorily admitted to hospital. As indicated above, such interruptions of fishing trips can be very expensive. They are classified as psychiatric disembarkations and Table 5.3 shows their contribution to all medical disembarkations, and the contribution, where it has

Table 5.3: The Contribution of Psychiatric Illness and Alcohol-related Psychiatric Illness to Medical Disembarkations of Fishing Vessels

	Per cent of all medical disembarkations		
	Psychiatric illness, including alcoholism	All alcohol-related psychiatric illness	Delirium tremens
Faroese Hospitals[1] n = 45	25	20	20
Gilbert Bain Hospital, Lerwick, Shetland[2] n = 78	17	8*	4
Hull deep-sea fishing fleet[3] n = 475	16	not known	not known
Scrabster, Caithness[4] n = 372	9	5	2

*This may be an underestimate since one case of paranoia occurred in a heavy drinker.
[1] Mair (1979).
[2] Cadenhead (1976).
[3] Richardson (1979).
[4] Mair and Deans (1979).

been identified, of alcohol-related psychiatric illness to all medical disembarkations.

It is possible that the increased accident rate which occurs during the first day at sea on side-winding trawlers (Richardson, 1979; Figure 5.1) is related to alcohol withdrawal as well as alcohol intoxication.

Drinking at Sea

The hospital records of the fishermen did not refer to many consequences of their drinking at sea although some of these can be inferred. One man who described himself as 'frequently helpless with drink until three days out of port' can hardly have performed his work satisfactorily. The records of many of the fishermen referred to accidents at sea, but in only one instance did they indicate that these had occurred to the fisherman while he had been under the influence of alcohol. Although many accidents at sea are probably alcohol-related there are many other factors in operation at sea which increase the risk of accidents.

Three men had been 'paid off' or suspended for being drunk at sea and it is reasonable to suppose that drinking may have had some part in the offence of a 20-year-old alcoholic who had spent a year in prison for piracy.

More serious acts of indiscipline may also be alcohol-related. In 1975 the High Court in Inverness witnessed the trial of a fisherman who killed his skipper at sea with a carving knife during a drunken argument (Aberdeen *Press and Journal*, 18 June 1975). During the trial the court heard of trawlermen drinking vodka, whisky, wine and beer as they made for the west coast fishing grounds off Lewis. The skipper who died had been drinking as well. At the time of the offence the accused was suspended without time limit by the Aberdeen Port Disciplinary Committee for assaulting the mate on another trawler, but he had been allowed to sail while his appeal was being considered.

Tackling the Problem

It is certain that alcoholics do exist in the fishing industry and they are entitled to some assistance in overcoming their dependence on alcohol or other alcohol-related problems. There is ample evidence that the fishing industry provides conditions which may encourage the heavy drinking which carries a risk of alcohol-related problems and dependence. These same conditions probably also attract to the industry a number of men who are either established alcoholics or predisposed to alcoholism. Therefore, there appear to be three main approaches to the problem: prevent alcoholics and those so predisposed from entering the industry; prevent the development of alcoholism in men already in the industry; and detect and offer assistance to those men in the industry who are alcoholic or becoming so.

Keeping Alcoholics out of the Industry

Although this study has pointed to certain factors which may predispose to alcoholism and which exist before men enter the fishing industry, not all of them are easily assessed in recruits, nor would it be desirable for men to be discriminated against on the basis of such assessments.

Some men may be at increased risk of alcoholism because they have a family history of alcoholism. In only a minority of recruits is such personal information likely to be available to prospective employers and even if it is available there are serious objections to rejecting recruits who have a familial background of alcoholism. Leaving aside the moral objections, there is a purely statistical one. The risk of alcoholism in the offspring of alcoholics was found in one study to be about 33 per cent (Goodwin *et al.*, 1973) so discrimination on this ground alone would result in two men not at risk of alcoholism being rejected for every one at such risk.

The situation is equally difficult in relation to personality disorder. We have even less idea what proportion of men with personality disorder are at risk of alcoholism and even if such information was available the likelihood of adequately assessing the presence or degree of personality disorder at recruitment is quite small.

Thus we are left with the possibility of detecting men who are already dependent on alcohol or exhibit alcohol-related problems. This appears to be practical to a certain degree, it is in the interests of the industry, and, in so far as one would not want to expose someone to conditions which would be likely to aggravate an existing or developing health problem, it is also in the interests of the potential recruit.

The likelihood of detecting alcohol dependence and alcohol-related problems depends to a large extent on the quality of information obtained when a medical and social history is taken and a physical examination carried out. This provides the opportunity for taking a drinking history as part of a general health and social history but the likelihood of the drinking history being unreliable is great. Physical examination, supplemented where indicated by laboratory investigations, may reveal evidence of alcohol-related pathology. While new entrants to the fishing industry are subjected to medical examinations in the four large fishing ports of Grimsby, Hull, Aberdeen and Fleetwood, they do not take place routinely in the smaller ports and this suggests an area for improvement.

Previous employment in occupations which also have a high risk of alcoholism should make the prospective employer suspicious and more so if the applicant's references indicate that the work-record was poor or that there were problems of discipline. The man's admitted record of criminal convictions, if reliable, should be similarly informative.

Having once entered the industry, the alcoholic may stay longer than would otherwise be the case because it is so easy to move about within the industry from one company to another. There are many improvements which could be made in this area. Disciplinary committees should not be limited to just the larger ports. Penalties imposed in one port should be enforced in other ports so that a man who is banned in one port is effectively banned throughout the industry. When a man moves from one company to another his disciplinary record should be available to the new employer.

Stopping the Development of Alcoholism in the Industry

While the relative importance of various aspects of the job milieu in promoting alcoholism in fishermen has not been quantified, attempts to eradicate or improve some of these features of the fishermen's life seem desirable in the broader interests of occupational health as well as in order to reduce the risk of alcoholism.

The availability of alcohol at work is one of the most tangible of such features of the fisherman's life, yet the experience of many years has shown that it is exceedingly difficult to control. Customs and merchant shipping regulations are desirable although their value is limited. The new Merchant Shipping Act (1979) provides for fines of up to £1,000 or two years imprisonment or both for persons convicted of taking unauthorised liquor on board fishing vessels or permitting another person to do so. It remains to be seen if such measures, and their means of enforcement, will be enough to reduce the availability of illicit alcohol on fishing vessels.

It is not simply a question of the availability of alcohol but of the way alcohol is used. The Department of Trade Working Group (1975) recommended that Section 28 of the Merchant Shipping Act (1970), which makes it an offence for a seaman to be on duty while under the influence of alcohol, should be extended to make it an offence for a fisherman to be on board a fishing vessel in a similar state. This has now been implemented in the new Merchant Shipping Act (1979). Complementary measures have also been suggested (Board of Trade, 1969; Department of Trade, 1975). These include the provision of a bar on large distant-water vessels, under the supervision of the skipper or other responsible officer, which, it is claimed, would remove the incentive for concentrated drinking early in the voyage if this was used as a means of rationing the alcohol. The Hull freezer trawler *Dane* is already experimenting with such a measure and each man can buy two cans of beer and a measure of spirits each night from the bar.

It is difficult to counter the social pressure to drink which exists in the fisherman's environment, since altering the availability and use of alcohol at sea is likely to have little impact on the drinking habits of

the fishermen on shore. What is required here, and in relation to many
of the recommendations, is a change of attitudes towards the use of
alcohol. Such changes take decades, if not centuries, to occur and,
although the likely effectiveness is not known, it seems reasonable to
suggest that new entrants to the industry should receive, during their
training, both theoretical and practical training concerning the use
and abuse of alcohol in the fishing industry with special reference to
discipline, safety and occupational health. This training should start
in the Trawl Apprentices' Schools and it should be reinforced by the
skippers and officers of vessels which carry deck learners.

Such a change in attitudes might tend to lessen the collusion and
permissiveness which characterise not only the practices of some
officers and crewmen but also some vessel owners. The new Merchant
Shipping Act (1979) details some of the powers which may be used
by ships' owners, masters and officers in relation to the taking of
unauthorised liquor aboard. These powers can be used by mercantile
marine superintendents and specially-appointed inspectors but it is
particularly important that regulations are seen to be enforced by
vessel owners and officers. The need for such enforcement applies
to other offences, whether or not alcohol-related, and it is a matter
of grave concern that the enforcement of such regulations should be
jeopardised by virtue of some skippers themselves being alcoholic.

There are few realistic measures likely to counter the separation
from normal social and sexual relationships, but particularly on
larger vessels it should be possible to provide diversions which lessen
the boredom. The exhibition of 'blue movies' has been suggested but
the facilities for showing films are available only on some of the
new stern-trawlers and they are not available on the older side-trawlers
and smaller vessels.

This century has already seen a vast improvement in the techno-
logy of fishing and although some of the improvements have reduced
the psychological and physical discomforts of the fisherman's life, the
occupation remains one of the most hazardous and uncomfortable in
the world. Every attempt must be made to reduce these discomforts
further.

The casual nature of the fisherman's employment calls for some
improvement and efforts must be made to stabilise the labour force
and provide some guarantee of continuing employment and wages. Such
improvements, referred to as 'decasualisation', were introduced in
August 1979.

Helping Alcoholic Fishermen

The success of most employee alcoholism programs hinges upon what is known as 'constructive coercion', which is the term used to describe the way in which the threat of dismissal is used to motivate the employee to obtain help in overcoming his alcoholism. Up to the time of writing it has not been possible to apply this principle to the fishing industry in view of the fact that the fisherman's employment has ceased anyway at the end of each fishing trip. However, the introduction of decasusalisation on 1 August 1979, provides new opportunities for the development of employee alcoholism programs in the fishing industry. Furthermore, now that the Merchant Shipping Act (1979) gives the Secretary of State in the Department of Trade power to make regulations '(a) for securing the safety of ships and persons on ships; (b) for protecting the health of persons on ships;' it might be possible, if owners and unions were in agreement, to use this power to make regulations which required the owners of vessels to establish and implement employee alcoholism programs. Powerful trade unions, convinced that such programs would be in the best interests of their members, non-alcoholic as well as alcoholic, ought to be able to stimulate the consideration of such a development.

The implementation of employee alcoholism programs would be greatly facilitated by the existence of satisfactory occupational health services for fishermen. The rationale for such a service was suggested by Moore (1969b): 'the establishment of an occupational health service for trawlermen with compulsory pre-employment and periodic examination would help to prevent unfit men going to sea and ensure that those sailing were of good health and not a liability to their fellows'. Detailed proposals for such a service were made by the Committee of Inquiry into Trawler Safety (Board of Trade, 1969):

(1) Occupational health services for fishermen should be extended to all ports and increased in scope.
(2) In the larger ports there is justification for employing a doctor on a full-time basis.
(3) The doctor should be well-qualified to undertake the work.
(4) Medical examination of all new entrants should be compulsory.
(5) All men off work due to sickness or injury must be examined before being allowed to return to sea.
(6) Older men should be subject to regular medical examinations.

Mair (1979) has examined the extent to which these proposals have been implemented and he has found that only the full-time

occupational health services of the Hull and Grimsby fleets satisfy
these recommendations. Aberdeen has no regular screening of older
men, nor does its service examine all previously ill men before allowing
them to return to sea. Fleetwood's service has no regular screening of
older men and it does not keep records of any sort. The inadequacy of
the Aberdeen and Fleetwood services is suggested by the finding that
in medical disembarkations of fishermen in Faroese hospitals there
was a significantly higher proportion of patients with a relevant
previous medical history from Fleetwood and Aberdeen compared
with Hull and Grimsby, suggesting a failure of the former two ports
to prevent medically-unfit men from going to sea. Consistent with
this finding is the observation that Aberdeen men were more common
than Grimsby and Hull men in medical disembarkations at Faroese
hospitals. While the possibility has to be considered that Aberdeen
boats fish in Faroese waters more than Hull and Grimsby boats,
this observation could also reflect the failure of the Aberdeen
trawlermen's health service to detect men who were medically unfit
to go to sea. Such a failure of the Aberdeen trawlermen's health
service is also suggested by the evidence from the hospital case records
of north-east Scotland fishermen which indicate that men were able to
return to sea immediately after unsuccessful treatment for alcoholism.

If all of the recommendations for an occupational health service
in the fishing industry were implemented throughout the industry,
this measure alone might result in the successful detection and rehabilitation of some of the industry's alcoholic employees.

Further opportunities for helping alcoholic fishermen could result
from the adaptation of some of the industry's disciplinary procedures.
It is likely that many alcoholic fishermen breach disciplinary
regulations. Some offences are referred to the local port disciplinary
committees while offences under the Merchant Shipping Acts are
dealt with through the courts. In either case if it is suspected that
alcohol is involved in an offence, or if it is not a first offence, the
committees and courts should have the power to defer sentence while
a medical report is obtained. If such a report indicated that there was
an underlying problem related to alcohol, the committee or court
should be able to defer sentence further if the fisherman wished to
seek help in overcoming his problem. He would be banned from
sailing while the report was obtained and while he obtained treatment.
He would not be allowed to sail again unless the committee or court
received evidence that his problem had been overcome. The success
of this procedure for assisting alcoholic fishermen would hinge upon

three important factors: (1) the stringent enforcement of disciplinary regulations; (2) the establishment of disciplinary committees to cover all the fishing ports with reciprocal arrangements between them; and (3) the existence of an occupational health service employing doctors who are skilled in the assessment of alcohol-related problems and who are fully aware of the nature and extent of the local services which could be used in order to rehabilitate successfully the alcoholic fisherman.

Conclusions

Research based on the study of hospital records has many limitations, particularly when the records relate to people, circumstances and events some ten years ago. Nevertheless, even this limited view of alcoholics in the fishing industry sheds some useful light on the relationship between occupation and alcoholism, particularly when placed in the context of the wider literature on the health, safety and social aspects of the occupation of fishing.

What happens to these fishermen is both an humanitarian and an economic concern. They put not only their own health and safety at risk, but also the health and safety of their ship-mates and the crews of other vessels at sea. Many are likely to constitute serious financial liabilities for reasons which have been discussed.

The fishing industry has already more than hinted at one method of dealing with its alcohol problem:

> If the boozers want it spelled out for them, may we pass on the comment that has been made to us several times recently from all sides of the industry. Namely, that if we are faced with any contraction of the industry in this coming year then we all know where to look for our 'reducible minority'. (*Trawling Times*, January 1975)

It is to be hoped that the trade unions and owners will come to regard such an approach as unacceptable, and look for other, more humane, methods of tackling the problem.

At present the fishing industry is faced with a number of problems. There is a steady decline in the size of the workforce and the size of the fishing fleets. The size of the catch on individual vessels has also been declining. This is partly a reflection of the lack of a common fisheries policy which ensures conservation of fish stocks, but it also reflects

EEC legislation which prohibits British vessels from certain fishing grounds and permits foreign boats to have access to what were exclusively British fishing grounds. It would be a pity if these problems caused the industry to overlook its alcohol problem, especially when the successful resolution of the problem could improve productivity and morale which are now even more important in the context of the industry's other problems.

Further research is required to elucidate properly the problems of the alcoholic in the fishing industry. Even so, there ought to be no delay in the industry, its insurers, the trade unions and the responsible government departments setting up a working party to examine the industry's alcohol problem and investigate possible solutions.

Acknowledgements

I am grateful to Mr David Hunter and Dr Peter Olley of the Clinical Research Unit, Royal Cornhill Hospital, and Department of Mental Health, University of Aberdeen, for enabling me to carry out the study of the hospital records. Dr W.T. Richardson, Medical Adviser to the UK Trawlers Mutual Insurance Company Limited, has kindly provided me with unpublished results of his own research relating to the Hull fishing fleet. Professor Alex Mair, Department of Community and Occupational Medicine, University of Dundee, has not only allowed me to include results of his own unpublished studies, but he has also assisted greatly by giving valuable comments on drafts of this chapter. I am grateful to Sheriff A.M.G. Russell, QC, of Aberdeen who assisted me in obtaining information concerning the legal proceedings which resulted from the collision between the *Leswood* and *Adastra*. Finally, I express my thanks to the Department of Trade officials who also provided valuable comments on earlier drafts.

Note

1. Verse 2:
    We shipped on the *Alaska* lying out in the bay
    Awaiting for a fair wind to get under way
    The sailors all drunk and their backs is all sore
    Their whiskey's all gone and they can't get no more.
(Reproduced by permission of Tiparm Music Publishers Inc.)

6 ALCOHOL AND OCCUPATION

Jacques Godard

It was not until the beginning of the eighteenth century, the age of enlightenment, that an Italian doctor Ramazzini suggested adding the question 'What is your profession?' to Hippocrates' famous classical list. More than 20 centuries were thus needed before the vast majority of doctors came to consider occupation in relation to illness.

Moreover, it was only around 1850 that the Swedish doctor Magnus Huss spoke for the first time about alcoholism. This term was immediately accepted amongst medical circles and from that time onwards increasing numbers of studies were carried out in relation to illness connected with the excessive consumption to alchool.

An Archaic Concept

At that time it must be remembered that the task was fairly simple. Excessive drinking was regarded as a moral rather than a health problem and doctors for their part were merely expected to look after the serious or often terminal complications of alcoholism. The prevailing attitude of society was first to mock and laugh at the buffoonery of the drunk, and then to rid itself of the problem as soon as the social limits of tolerance had been exhausted and it became too dangerous or burdensome to bear.

The solution was what a contemporary French philosopher Michel Foucault called 'the great confinement'. Depending on the main aspects of the immoral behaviour, the unfortunate individual was either deemed mad and sent to a lunatic asylum, or guilty and put in prison. Indeed, the question of prevention or treatment of alcoholism never arose and drunkenness was in no way considered to be the concern of doctors. Rather it was regarded as a vice or an unpardonable scandal. At the very best, certain charitable people believed that for every sin there was to be found mercy, their duty being therefore to take pity on these poor souls heading for damnation and to endeavour to 'raise' them.

Moreover, in the course of the nineteenth century the notion of vice was often accompanied by the idea of deficiency, and was considered

more or less as hereditary and to be found only amonst the lowest
strata and the most deprived of the society. As one humorist put it,
beyond a certain income one is no longer an alcoholic but rather an
'ethylic', which sounded much more distinguished.

But despite this, evils resulting from alcohol use were nonetheless
described in impressively realistic terms. An abundant literature has
been devoted to this amongst which can be found such famous
authors as Dostoyevsky, Dickens and Zola as well as many others.
In particular, since the Second World War the work of Jellinek,
Fouquet and others under the auspices of the World Health Organisation
has enabled the concept of alcoholism as an illness to emerge from the
mythical and moralising stance in which it has been trapped for
centuries of prejudices and tradition. Little interest was taken until
recently in the relationship of alcoholism and work. This includes both
the influence of excessive consumption of alcohol on work, and the
influence of work on excessive consumption of alcohol. Further
examination is necessary of the interaction of alcohol with compounds
existing at the workplace.

The Influence of Excessive Consumption of Alcohol on Work

This aspect of alcoholism has only been examined in the last few
decades and has been studied particularly in the United States and in
France, other countries having made few references to the subject
except where it concerns traffic accidents. There are two main reasons
why these studies should have been centred in France.

An Important Heritage

First, alcohol consumption is particularly high in France. Indeed it is
the country with the highest alcohol production in relation to its
population. Moreover it is one of the countries which became con-
scious of the problem at a very early stage, particularly amongst the
managerial, political, scientific, economic and medical professions. It
must be remembered that it *was as early as 1872* that the first association for the prevention of alcoholism was founded in France. Amongst
the names of the eminent people who took this initiative is to be found
that of Louis Pasteur. It is also in this country that since the beginning
of the century and in particular from 1954 onwards, the most diverse
measures have been taken to limit this evil. Have these been at least
partially effective?

It is perhaps presumptuous at this stage to say so. It remains true that the average consumption of alcohol per inhabitant and mortality caused by alcoholic cirrhosis is particularly high in France. Nevertheless it can be shown that there are signs that the trend is being reversed — whilst in many other countries such indicators are on the increase. Thus, despite a precarious and dangerous situation, awareness in France of the problems of alcohol remains and indeed has become more acute. For this reason numerous attempts have been made to analyse the situation.

An Original Law on the Implication of Work and Health

The second determining factor which favoured research in this field was the simple fact that in 1942 extremely original legislation on health and work was laid down in France.

While the first doctors to intervene at the work premises were, for example, casualty officers in the United States and Sweden and toxicologists in Germany, and while in the majority of industrialised countries the emphasis was put on hygiene and safety, in the workshops of France the situation was somewhat different. Though not neglecting these aspects French legislation also stressed the need *for a careful surveillance of the individual health of the workers.*

The law of 11 October 1946 outlines these principles and states the following in its first article:

The services of medicine at work are guaranteed by one or more doctors hereby named physicians at work. Their role is exclusively preventive; to avoid any change in the health of the workers caused as a result of their work, in particular by watching the hygienic conditions at work, the risks of contagion and the state of health of the workers.

It was this last point which was original. For, in effect, these French regulations provided for compulsory health examinations at least once a year. This was to be obligatory for all employees and not merely for those threatened by particular professional hazards. A group of physicians was thus established, paid by the employers, who had to see to it that each worker could remain on the job without risk either to himself or to his companions — in short, to make sure that he was fit for his job. Putting these principles into practice was inevitably not easy and many psychological and material problems were encountered and even the principle of such a practice was questioned. These

problems remain to this day. The role of the industrial physician is
difficult, since he sometimes has to take decisions which prove harmful
to certain interests, including those of the employee or the employer.

The Role of the Industrial Physician in the Field of Alcoholism

It must be emphasised that attentive physicians did not take long to
become aware of the damage caused by excessive alcohol to the
working population of the country. Certain of these doctors soon
made notes in their medical dossiers and communicated the results of
their observation to others. The main difficulty, however, lay in the
lack of a clinical definition of alcoholism and the lack of any objective
criteria which allowed them to assess the varying degrees of severity.

The first attempts at research were therefore pragmatic. A particularly
striking example occurred in about 1955. At this time the industrial
physicians in a region of east France were asked to estimate the percentage of workers in factories under their charge who suffered from
problems connected with alcohol consumption. The answers ranged from
one per cent to 14 per cent for doctors in charge of almost identical
working populations. This only went to show that these rates depended
much more on the subjective opinions of the practitioner than on
objective and common criteria.

The situation has developed appreciably since then. Three factors
have become increasingly important. First a considerable effort has
been made to improve the information available to the practitioners
on the subject and increase the general awareness of the problem. Then
there has been the frequent use of a check-list, well known in France
under its name of *Grid de Go* (Le Go and Pertusier, 1971). This enabled a systematic examination of the objective signs of alcoholism
even at a very early stage. Lastly there is the frequent use of laboratory
tests. These were, for the main part, reliable and the most important
consisted of measuring an increase in the rate of hepatic enzymes, such
as gamma glutamyl transpeptidase (γ $-GT$) and the increase in the
average blood count of red corpuscles (MCV).

Without going into detail of the discussions which followed the
establishment of these research techniques and which are still being
continued today, we must emphasise that this research went to confirm what empiricism and mere clinical examination had already
shown. That is to say if one compares a group of workers considered
as moderate drinkers or abstainers *de facto*, with a group of workers

doing exactly the same job but detected by industrial physicians as being excessive drinkers or drug addicts, the latter would be:

(1) more often absent due to illness;
(2) more often injured;
(3) would age prematurely and their efficiency both in personal and professional capacity would be reduced as a result;
(4) would die prematurely; and
(5) would have a disturbed social, professional and family life.

It stands to reason that those who have alcohol-related problems frequently suffer from incapacities resulting from alcohol, nor do they suffer the consequences alone. Let us now examine several examples.

Excessive Drinkers are Absent More Often due to Sickness

As early as 1950, it was noted in a certain factory in the region of Normandy that the number of days off work due to illness was on average 61.7 days per year for the 95 alcoholic subjects whilst only 33.5 for the 693 subjects known to be non-alcoholic.

Another Parisian study examined 15 people on prolonged sickness insurance benefit. Three were teetotallers, three only light drinkers, five confirmed alcoholics, one a heavy drinker and three were alcoholics suffering from mental disorder.

In a factory of public works in the Toulouse region which had 1,600 workers, Cavalie (1955) compared a group of 67 alcoholics with a group of 67 men of a similar professional standing. He followed their progress from 1951 to 1954 and found that amongst the first category absenteeism due to sickness was four times higher.

Godard, in 1954, in the course of a survey carried out amongst 35 serious alcoholic cases, noted that in one year the average absenteeism due to all causes was 49.4 out of 100 days work. This compares with only 8.9 days on average for the 4,500 employees in the same factory.

Haas (1971) ascertained that in a large automobile factory in Paris, absenteeism due to sickness amongst the alcoholic workers was some 4.4 times greater than that of the comparison group. This absenteeism was particularly apparent from the many sick alcoholics in the general male wards of the hospital.

Morbidity of Alcoholics

As early as 1952, Pequignot, in Paris, showed that in his practice of
Hotel Dieu, of the 636 men in the 40–69 year age group who were
taken into hospital in one year, 47.6 per cent were diagnosed as non-
alcoholics, 36.3 per cent were suffering from slight alcoholism, and
16.1 per cent were classified as alcoholic. Amongst the women of the
same age, the corresponding figures were 73 per cent, 14.4 per cent
and 12 per cent (Pequignot, 1955).

In Nantes, in the west of the country, Perrin (1960, 1961) found
that out of 1,121 patients in hospital between the ages of 40 to 60,
55 per cent were alcoholic. For the 518 women the figure was 32 per
cent.

Lereboullet of Paris (1972) found that for a Paris hospital the
alcoholic stayed for 45 days while the average for a non-alcoholic was
only 21 days. The average cost for the hospital stay was (in 1967)
6,600 francs for those suffering from cirrhosis (70 days), 5,055 francs
for chronic alcoholics (64 days), while only 1,209 francs for non-
alcoholics (21 days). Indeed one could not choose a better example
to show the cost of alcoholism to the French social security system
and indeed for all French tax-payers.

Of particular interest is a study carried out by Arnoux (1972) in a
hospital in the south-east of the country at Carpentree, a small city
not far from Avignon. Here he showed that one out of every three
men in the adult medical wards of the hospital were suffering from
alcoholism. In surgical cases, the proportion was one out of every
five. It must be stressed that this particular city is in the Department
of Vaucluse, a wine-growing area and considered as being one of the
areas most affected by alcoholism.

In French psychiatric hospitals the percentage of admissions to
hospital for alcoholism was 22 per cent before the war; this fell to
11.9 per cent in 1944 and then rose again to 42.2 per cent. At
present the figures stand at 36 per cent for men and 8 per cent for
women.

Finally, one must point out the harmful effect of alcohol on
pregnancy and maternity. Here again there is a relationship between
the behaviour of the alcoholic female and absenteeism.

Excessive Drinkers are Those Most Often Injured

For a long time a number of surgeons have noted the frequency of
acute or chronic alcoholism amongst the victims of surgical injury.

Professor Quenu (1955) of Paris noted that out of 100 injured in
his practice, 32 had a blood level of alcohol above 1 g/l, while Morice
(1954) of Caen in Normandy noted that 48 per cent of the patients
hospitalised for accidents at work showed evident signs of alcoholism.
This compared with an average of some 18 per cent for workers in
the surrounding factories fulfilling the same criteria. An important
study was carried out on a sample of more than 5,000 people by
Metz and Marcoux in Strasbourg in 1960 with the assistance of eight
industrial physicians. Here it was apparent that at least 15 per cent
of the accidents could be ascribed to alcohol (Metz and Marcoux,
1960). Moreover, subjects with an alcohol level above 0.25 g/l
were found to be twice as likely to have suffered from more than
one accident. Finally, in the Paris region, Haas (1970) found 3.55 times
more accidents amongst a group of alcoholics.

As for road accidents, endless statistical studies have shown both
in France and in other countries that 30—50 per cent of serious and
fatal accidents are due to alcohol. A recent survey (1975) carried out
by Professor Got in the western suburbs of Paris showed undeniably
that a state of alcohol intoxication was to be found in 38 per cent of
accident cases either in the party at fault or the victim of the accident
— given that the person responsible and the victim might often be
the same person. This level reached 52 per cent between 6 p.m. and
3 a.m. and even 60 per cent on Sunday evening.

**Excessive Drinkers Age Prematurely and their Working Capability
Suffers as a Result**

Today, human work, even if it is monotonous and repetitive, makes
increasing demands on the mind and on the senses, and decisions
must be taken at all levels in the workforce. Physical strength is now
less important, but vigilance, quick reflexes and clear judgement are
becoming more and more necessary. An example which can be given
to show this trend is the work done by the manual worker of bygone
days compared with that of the driver of a bulldozer today.

It is now increasingly apparent that excessive drinkers are, in
varying degrees, particularly inept for many jobs. In this sense it

could be said that alcoholism is an 'anachronistic evil' (Alfred Sauvy, 1971). Fontan of Lille noted that there was a marked deterioration in the intellectual faculties of excessive drinkers from the ages of 40–50 onwards. Desanti and Aillaud (1971) described how amongst a large population of national insurance members in Marseille there was a marked deterioration of physical and intellectual aptitude in the excessive consumer.

Godard, Durrmeyer and Delabroise (1966) noted that about 40 per cent of the changes of jobs in the steel industry due to work ineptitude concerned alcoholics. Another piece of research showed that in 1972 some 30 per cent of those who retired early were obvious drinkers, and in 1967 J.M. Le Go showed that 38 per cent of railway employees dismissed for illness, were dismissed due to alcoholism.

Lastly, consider an intriguing study undertaken by Bresard in St Etienne in 1971, when he showed that alcoholism acted as a break on social promotion. The sons of employees who had slipped down the social hierarchy consumed some 50 per cent more alcohol than those who had risen successfully. Those who remained in the same position consumed 29 per cent more alcohol than those who had benefited from promotion.

This then is the picture of a worker, exhausted, whose status is lowered in the eyes of the world and who is prematurely aging due to alcoholism which is seldom brought out in the open. And yet it appears to constitute an extremely heavy burden on society as a whole.

Excessive Drinkers Die Prematurely

The chronic ill health which we have just described is usually the first stage on the way to a premature death. Ledermann showed in 1956 that the well-known higher rate of mortality amongst middle-aged men as compared to women was particularly accentuated in countries which experienced heavy alcohol consumption, e.g. in France where the rate of mortality is at present 2.5 times greater amongst men than amongst women aged between 40 to 50. Research carried out since then by various authors has also shown the important part played by alcohol and nicotine poisoning.

Godard (1955) noted that in a working population of 4,500 employees in the east of France, 51 per cent of deaths occuring before retirement age were due, whatever the official cause stated, to employees suffering from alcoholism. Yet the incidence of alcoholism in the total population was in the order of 10—15 per cent. It must be stated that amongst the many diagnoses established at the time of death, there was frequently a direct or aggravating factor of excessive alcohol consumption. This, however, nearly always remained hidden simply because it was not declared.

Gervois and Dubois (1977) at Lille, showed recently that the life expectations for an excessive drinker aged 25 years was reduced on average by 12 years. Meanwhile Niveau (1977) showed somewhat to his surprise that in a particular mining community the average age of death amongst alcoholics was lower than those disabled through silicosis.

Excessive Drinkers Disturb the Normal Functioning of Social, Family and Professional Life

The above statement undoubtedly holds true although in this chapter we are concentrating on professional life. As yet, no detailed study has been carried out on this subject. Nevertheless, one can assume that the presence at work of people who are more or less ill, frequently absent, physically or mentally disturbed, with difficult characters, liable to unforseeable and dangerous actions, whose productivity is low, and who are frequently responsible for accidents, breakages and bad workmanship must undoubtedly create many difficulties—whether this be on an individual or personal level.

It would be wrong to believe that studies, carried out to show the importance of this situation, are aiming in any way to criticise alcoholics, to place them in a yet more difficult situation *vis a vis* their bosses and companions or to engender a sense of guilt amongst them. Rather, it is an attempt to make the public as aware as possible of the dangers of alcohol, its far-reaching influence and the need to prevent, detect and treat these individuals.

The Influence of Work on the Excessive Consumption of Alcohol

Because of the interdependence between an individual or a group and the environment, one must now consider what might be the effect of the physical and psychological conditions of the workplace on the level of alcohol consumption.

Tiredness

Amongst the many physical considerations there is no doubt that tiredness encourages excessive drinking. Obviously, an outlay of human energy leads to muscular fatigue and dehydration. This is particularly true if a lot of energy is expended and this is done in uncomfortably hot conditions or in an atmosphere which is dusty, noxious or too dry. Certain research (Lehman (1955) in West Germany and Metz (1964) in France) has shown that dehydration can, in some tasks, in particular in the mines and steel industry, result in up to four to six litres of water being lost per day by each worker (Metz, 1964).

Replacement of this loss by alcoholic beverages leads to problems of excretion through the kidney. Alcohol is a diuretic — the more alcohol one drinks, the more thirsty one becomes and the more drunk therefore one becomes as a result. On the other hand, it is well-known that initially alcohol produces a sense of euphoria and excitement, and to a certain extent acts as an anaesthetic (drunk people do not suffer so much when they hurt themselves). Thus, although the muscular and psychic senses are weakened as has been shown by many different tests, nevertheless the subject in a state of intoxication feels himself and believes himself to be more robust and more competent.

It is amongst the workers who are the most exhausted and thirsty that the risk of excessive drinking is greatest, during, as well as after, work. Certain professions have been and still are particularly affected in this way — metal workers, miners, sailors, dockers, cooks and general unskilled labourers — many of whom are foreign and stateless and live in deplorable moral and material conditions.

Co-toxicity (Interaction of Alcohol with Other Substances)

Recently the potential effects of alcohol on certain pharmacological products and their functioning are beginning to be studied in depth. For example, it appears that neuroleptics, hypnotics, etc. reinforce the effects alcohol has on the nervous system, whilst in other cases it is the increased rate at which antibiotics, antiparasitics and reserpine are absorbed into the intestine in association with alcohol that leads to unfortunate consequences. Another mechanism might be the fact that the process of alcohol metabolism is blocked, as for example with the effect of disulfiram or Antabuse.

But, in the field of industrial toxicity, it must be recognised that we are still in a state of ignorance although it is definitely known, for example, that calcium carbimide has a considerably increased effect when mixed with alcohol, a similar effect to Antabuse. Similarly it is known that certain products, benzol, chlorethylene carbon disulphide, and in general all fat solvents, reinforce the effect alcohol has on nervous tissue. Some believe that slight intoxication from industrial compounds such as lead, arsenic and aniline, could on the one hand lead to a certain craving for alcohol, while on the other make the subject more sensitive to the poison. Moreover, the combined effect of carbon monoxide and alcohol might explain accidents, particularly those concerning drivers of heavy loads. However, as yet one can only state that far too little research has been carried out in the vast areas of toxicology.

Psycho-social Factors at Work Affecting Drinking Behaviour

First of all, one must mention that in countries where consumption of wine is important, there is a time-honoured custom of offering one's visitors, tradesmen and indeed all workers something to drink. Naturally, the traditional forms of politeness make it only possible to drink to someone's health if one's glass contains alcohol, and in some sense this makes the event sacred.

These customs are observed in a wide range of professions, indeed from the most modest to the highest positions in society, their common trait lying in the fact that they concern working relationships. No social category can escape this, from dustmen, postmen, commercial travellers and door-to-door salesmen to presidents and managers obliged to hold business lunches. Priests and doctors are professionals with a high alcoholic risk who also fall into this category. A study of these contemporary customs would be desirable, and intensive education should be undertaken in those areas in which these traditions persist.

Next, even the nature of work may have a part to play. Monotony and solitude characterise many jobs in the modern world, and boredom all too often leads to persistent drinking. Similar effects result from the changes in hours of work and night work. Together with several colleagues Godard (1964) noted that the consumption of alcoholic beverages as well as of tobacco and coffee was greater during the week of night work for those workers who practiced alternate shifts.

Jobs which relate to the production and sale of alcohol are also generally considered as professions having a high risk. However in relation to this also, we lack detailed studies since too many conflicting interests have managed to obscure the true picture.

Lastly, as we have already mentioned, though modern work may demand less physical effort it is often more taxing mentally. Indeed, it frequently demands a greater concentration, speedy and varied reactions and more intense mental effort. All of these can lead to excessive stress. Certain recognised studies, for example on switchboard operators, have shown this clearly.

Thus, though alcohol may act as a pleasant relaxant and as an anaesthetic reducing temporarily a state of nervous tension, at the same time it can lead to a dangerous alcohol dependence.

Differing Alcoholism Rates in Differing Occupations

It is commonplace to say that humans are not all affected in the same way by alcohol and the same can be said to apply for occupations. Certain occupations are of high risk in relation to alcoholism.

A survey, responded to by nearly 400 industrial physicians and covering a work population of some 900,000 employees showed clearly the considerable differences in the frequency of pathological states related to alcohol in different occupations. These results were presented in 1969. Table 6.1 shows certain examples of the frequency of alcoholism recognised by the physicians.

As we have already stressed, the percentages in this table must be approached with certain care, but important progress has been made for some years in the field of detection, and these studies provide more or less reliable indications.

At first it seems hard to accept the fact that in one company some 30—40 per cent of workers who have been recruited might be pre-disposed to excessive consumption of alcohol, whilst elsewhere the figure might be only one per cent, even if one admits, as one must, the importance of other factors such as social milieu, qualifications, average age and region. Above all, one factor must be stressed: that is the quality of inter-human relationships within the company.

Frequently we have observed obvious cases of alcoholic 'contagion' where the old bosses in the offices or foremen lure their young colleagues into drinking, particularly at the end of the working day. This will in its turn lead to the younger ones in some years time also becoming alcoholics. Thus the company could either represent a pro-tected or a dangerous environment and this will depend on the behaviour of the bosses throughout the company, the shop stewards, the medical and social services, and the organisation of the work. Other considerations which must not be ignored are the conditions of health, hygiene and work, and the type of human

Table 6.1: Examples of Frequency of Alcoholism Recognised by Hospitals*

Occupation	Frequency (%)
Computer centre (Paris)	0.20
Banking group (Paris)	0.65
Electronic factory (the Paris region)	1
Hospital centre (the west-central region)	2.5
Transport company (central region):	
drivers	4.15
factory workers	10.26
Metal company (central region):	
professional workers	5
unqualified workers	9.7
Metal factory (north region)	10
Mines (northern region)	13
Metal company (western region):	
according to shop floor	15–30
Metal company (south-eastern region)	23
Inter-company medical services (west):	
according to company	5–22
Building and public works (eastern region)	30–40

*There were also three cases of delirium tremens for 60 occupational groups in one year.

relationships which exists.

Conclusions

I am perfectly aware that this chapter applies to a particular case, that of French industry in general (in a country where wine consumption is high), and especially to a sector which was for a long time my field of observation — that of the large metal industry in the east of France. Certain important changes would certainly have to be made if it were to apply to other countries and it would also be important to include toxins other than alcohol, but the principle would still hold true: in any analysis of the aetiological factors of alcoholism, the environment of the workplace must be included.

7 PROBLEM DRINKING AMONG AMERICAN RAILROAD WORKERS

F. James Seaman

Background

Many of the estimated ten million American adults (Department of Health, Education and Welfare, 1978) with drinking problems hold jobs (Schramm, Mandell and Archer, 1978). Recent studies of the prevalence of alcohol-related problems at work have yielded varying prevalance rates. This variability can be traced to different operational definitions of the problem, different drinking behaviour among various workforces, and the use of questionable methods for deriving estimates (Reynolds, Mannello and Seaman, 1978). Increasing evidence indicates, nevertheless, that drinking is a serious problem in many industries and that problem drinking impairs job performance and productivity and consequently increases company costs (Observer and Maxwell, 1959; Trice, 1965a, b; Schramm, Mandell and Archer, 1978; Heyman, 1978).

Roman and Trice (1970) and, later, Trice and Roman (1972) hypothesised that several job factors may either lead a person to become a problem drinker, enable a person to hide his or her problem, or both. These factors include:

(1) Lack of visibility
   (a) jobs in which production goals are nebulous;
   (b) flexible work schedules and output permitting an individual to exercise options; and
   (c) jobs which are remote from direct observation by supervisors and work associates.
(2) Stress factors stemming from the absence of structured work
   (a) work addiction;
   (b) work role removal and occupational obsolescence; and
   (c) job roles novel to the organisation.
(3) Absence of social controls
   (a) jobs roles which require drinking as part of work role performance;
   (b) job roles in which one's deviant drinking benefits others in the organisation; and
   (c) moving from a job with social controls in which heavy

drinking is practised to release stress into a job in which such controls are absent.

Many of these factors come together in railroad jobs. Work crews are typically geographically-dispersed with little opportunity for observation by supervisors. The industry as a whole is shrinking. As jobs are eliminated and more railroads pass into receivership and bankruptcy, work-related stress increases. Moreover, there is a culture of drinking on the railroads; railroad workers, in general, have always been drinkers. If for no reason other than that the railroad population is predominantly male, one should expect that there are higher percentages of drinkers and problem drinkers in the railroad population than in the general population.

'A Major Train Accident'

Unlike many occupations, however, railroad work can often have far-ranging effects on the public at large.

At 12.45 a.m. on 25 June 1973, a Southern Pacific freight train collided with the rear end of another Southern Pacific freight train which was standing in the yard at Indio, California. The moving freight train consisted of five locomotives, 70 cars, and a caboose. Upon impact, the caboose of the stationary train was driven into and over the first locomotive of the colliding train. After hitting the caboose, the moving train continued forward, ploughing through the seven rear cars of the standing train. The fuel tanks of several of the locomotive units were punctured; diesel fuel sprayed over the wreckage and ignited. All five locomotive units and the first seven cars of the colliding train were derailed and destroyed. In addition, the thirty-first car and the ten cars behind it were derailed and heavily damaged as a result of the impact.

Eight cars of a freight train on an adjacent track were derailed and damaged when they were struck by the derailing equipment of the colliding train. The engineer and front brakeman of the moving train were killed. Five other individuals who were riding on the train sustained minor injuries. Damage to equipment and track was estimated to be $1.6 million. The cost of clearing the wrecks probably raised the total cost to over $2 million (about £1 million).

The National Transportation Safety Board (1974) concluded:

... that the probable cause of the accident was the failure of the crew ... to stop their train, which was being operated at excessive speed by an engineer under the influence of alcohol. Contributing to this failure was the ineffectiveness of the Southern Pacific in assuring compliance with its (own) operating rules and procedures which were specifically designed to prevent an accident if a crew-member failed to perform his duties. (p.2)

Among its recommendations, NTSB called on the Federal Railroad Administration (FRA) to issue regulations prohibiting employees from using narcotics and intoxicants while on duty and for a specified time before reporting on duty. All parties within the railroad industry concurred that action was required to avert a similar tragedy. Labour and management representatives indicated that they preferred to handle problems caused by employees using mind-altering drugs (including alcohol) voluntarily, through joint labour-management committees — not through new government regulations.

Drafts of initial regulations raised more questions than answers. The FRA decided to support the industry's voluntary efforts rather than to impose regulations. The rapid establishment of employee assistance programs demonstrated the railroad industry's willingness to address the problem. In order to encourage and assist such efforts, FRA let a contract to the University Research Corporation on Washington, D.C., to determine, among other things, the numbers of railroad workers having problems related to drinking, and the nature of those problems.

Method

Seven American Class 1 railroads agreed to participate in the study. Class 1 railroads are the largest in the country and are defined as those with operating revenues in excess of $10 million (roughly £5 million) per year. The seven railroads studied effectively cover the 48 contiguous states and employ half of all the workers employed by the Class 1 railroads. This amounts to approximately one-quarter of a million individuals.

Railroads agreed to provide access to various types of records and to allow approximately 30 interviews of key railroad personnel, including top- and middle-level management, labour leaders including general and local chairmen, first-line supervisors, the labour relations, safety and medical officers, and the directors and staff of the railroad employee assistance programs.

In addition, two anonymous sample surveys were conducted by mail on each of the seven railroads. The first of these was addressed to individuals who had encountered the company employee assistance programs and had either accepted or declined services. A major purpose of this survey was to evaluate the effectiveness of these programs and to determine corrective strategies to improve program services. The heart of the study, however, was another venture, a general survey of railroad personnel on each of the railroads and it is this survey which provides the data reported here.

Random samples of approximately 1,300 employees were drawn from the personnel files of each railroad. Samples were stratified and proportionately allocated according to type. This yielded three strata:

(1) *Exempt Employees* — non-union personnel including managers, administrators and professional staff;
(2) *Operating Crafts* — union personnel who serve on the train and engine while the train is moving; and
(3) *Non-operating Crafts* — union personnel who do not serve on the train while it is moving.

In most cases, results will be collapsed across railroads and strata except for where differences among those strata or railroads are particularly enlightening.

Results

Response rates for the seven study railroads range from 61 per cent to 83 per cent with a median of 70 per cent. Cases were weighted to compensate for differential response rates.

The figures reported here fall into three general areas:

(1) drinking on the job;
(2) drinking in general; and
(3) problems resulting from drinking.

Drinking on the Job

'Rule G' and other explicit and implicit rules make drinking on the job, reporting to work under the influence of alcohol and possessing alcoholic beverages on company property dismissable offences in the American rail industry. Still, we all know that rules are not always obeyed. It seems logical to ask therefore, how many workers have actually seen a co-worker drink while on duty? The numbers are shown in Table 7.1 and are quite high, ranging from 12 to 60 per cent with a median of 36 per cent. Although not shown in the table, these percentages remain high in all job categories, although they are a little lower for the exempt workers than for the contract employees.

Table 7.1: Percentage of Respondents Seeing a Co-worker Drink on Duty in the Past Year

Railroad	Percentage
1	36
2	47
3	12
4	30
5	28
6	60
7	36
Overall	35
Median	36

The numbers take on additional significance when one realises that another rule in the railroad industry, 'Rule C', makes it a dismissable offence not to report a witnessed violation of Rule G. Table 7.1 shows high percentages witnessing drinking on duty. These numbers probably exceed the actual incidence of drinking on duty, however, because more than one observer may see the same event. Other data from the survey indicate that the actual prevalence of on-the-job drinking ranges from four to 25 per cent with a prevalence for the entire sample of 12.3 per cent. Given the data of Table 7.1 indicating that so many railroad workers have had drinking co-workers, we can ask how serious that drinking has actually been. Is it just a beer with lunch or is it heavy drinking with potentially serious consequences?

Table 7.2 shows the percentages of workers on each railroad who in the past year have had co-workers too drunk or hungover to perform their jobs. When one considers the safety and cost factors associated with many railroad jobs, these numbers, too, seem frighteningly high. As the table shows, they range from nine to 21 per cent with a median

Table 7.2: Percentages of Workers Who Have Had Co-workers Too Drunk or Hungover to Perform in the Past Year

Railroad	Percentage
1	18
2	19
3	9
4	17
5	10
6	21
7	15
Overall	15
Median	17

of 17 per cent.

Even if the public is not being affected (and they probably are), a good percentage of co-workers are coming into contact with, and being influenced by, drinking railroad workers. How are they being influenced? Table 7.3 indicates, for one thing, that at least part of the time they are *scared*. Almost one-quarter are 'very often' afraid when a co-worker drinks; only about one-third are 'almost never' or 'never' afraid.

Table 7.4 shows some other consequences. It reports the reactions of individuals who have had a co-worker too drunk to perform adequately in the past year, i.e. the percentages which were reported in Table 7.2. Because the reactions are not mutually exclusive, the percentages total more than 100 per cent. At the top of the table, we see that over half got angry with the worker. As in many circumstances, in railroad work norms may say that it is permissible to drink but not to get drunk. This may be especially true because 60 per cent of these observers report having to work harder because of the co-worker's drunkenness. Only seven per cent seemed to react by working less hard

Table 7.3: Are You Ever Afraid When a Co-worker Drinks?

	Percentage
Very often	24
Often	11
Sometimes	31
Almost never	18
Never	16

Table 7.4: Effects of Co-worker Drinking

	Percentages
Got angry with drunk	53
Worked harder for drunk	60
Worked less hard	7
Hid the drinker	22
Told worker to go to EAP	15
Reported worker to boss	14
Told worker to go home	37

themselves. However, 22 per cent did actually hide the drunk co-worker to keep him or her out of trouble.

About one-sixth either reported the drunk co-worker to a boss or suggested that he or she go to the employee assistance program (EAP). Two-fifths just told the drunk co-worker to go home.

Table 7.5 shows the percentages of workers seeing various kinds of property damaged 'at least in part because a worker was drinking'. When one considers the cost (a locomotive costs several hundred thousand dollars) and the safety implications of damage to railroad equipment, many of these numbers are high enough to cause alarm.

Several points are worthy of note in this table. First, note the differences between railroads. Much more damage is being witnessed on Railroad 6, for example, than on Railroad 3. Also, note that the numbers are consistent for different kinds of equipment. The drinking is not just taking place on the trains or out along the line, but in the shops or in the offices as well. It occurs everywhere and therefore the

Table 7.5: Percentages of Workers Seeing Various Kinds of Equipment Damaged

Type of equipment	1	2	3	4	5	6	7	Overall
Trains	2	5	1	4	2	5	3	3
Track	2	3	1	2	2	2	3	2
Construction equipment	1	4	0	3	1	3	1	2
Buildings	2	6	1	6	2	6	2	3
Office equipment	2	4	1	2	1	4	2	2
Automobiles	3	4	0	3	1	4	2	3

damage is everywhere.

Thirdly, because of the way railroads are organised, not everyone is likely to see the same kinds of damage. For example, train and engine crews are unlikely to see typewriters or copying machines damaged and clerks are unlikely to see cars derail. This point is raised only to indicate that if railroads were organised differently, the numbers in Table 7.5 would be higher. Later analyses will look at these data again from the perspective of who is most likely to witness each kind of damage.

So far we have established that there are rules governing on-the-job drinking, that they are 'frequently' ignored, and that damage does result. Tables 7.6 and 7.7 indicate how serious the potential consequences of a worker's drinking would have to be before the respondent would report the drinking. The two tables are included to show the variation which exists in the standards among the roads. Clearly, the workers on Railroad 6 (Table 7.7) are more tolerant of problem drinking than those on Railroad 3 (Table 7.6).

Table 7.6: Percentage of Workers Willing to Report Given Certain Consequences (Railroad 3 — Southern US)

	Exempt	Ops*	Non-ops	Overall
Damage less than $50	89	67	67	72
Damage $50–$500	96	77	83	84
Damage more than $500	98	82	87	88
Self-injury	97	92	91	92
Injure another	100	97	96	97
Kill him/herself	100	94	95	96
Kill another	100	97	97	98
Bad decision	96	90	90	90

*See p. 121 for definitions

Apart from the actual numbers, several things in these tables are worthy of note:

(1) Exempt workers are consistently more likely to report than are contract workers.

(2) As the seriousness of consequences increases, the likelihood of reporting increases for all occupational categories and both railroads.

(3) If another worker is likely to be killed or injured rather than the drinker the likelihood of reporting is greater regardless of

Table 7.7: Percentage of Workers Willing to Report Given Certain Consequences (Railroad 6 – Northeastern US)

	Exempt	Ops	Non-ops	Overall
Damage less than $50	66	26	34	35
Damage $50–$500	84	42	53	53
Damage more than $500	87	54	62	62
Self-injury	87	73	73	74
Injure another	94	88	91	91
Kill him/herself	94	88	90	90
Kill another	95	92	93	93
Bad decision	90	71	73	74

railroad or occupational category.
(4) The data reflect known national trends: Southern workers (Railroad 3) are less tolerant of problem drinking than Northeastern workers (Railroad 6).

Drinking in General

Table 7.8 shows the percentages of workers who ever drank beverages containing alcohol and those who are current drinkers. The percentages of current drinkers range from 55 to 84 per cent with a median of 78 per cent. This figure is quite a bit higher than the national estimate of 67 per cent, but does not appreciably exceed the national estimate for men which is about 75 per cent (Johnson *et al.*, 1977).

Table 7.9 shows the prevalence of various consumption behaviours of the drinkers in the sample. A fair number are consuming

Table 7.8: Percentages of Drinkers among the Seven Workforces

Railroad	Percentage of Lifetime Drinkers	Percentage of Current Drinkers
1	94	84
2	91	80
3	73	55
4	92	78
5	85	69
6	92	84
7	89	75
Overall	88	75

Table 7.9: Various Consumption Behaviours of Drinkers in the Sample

	Percentage
Drink twice a day or more	3
Drank 2 6-packs at least once last month**	14
Drank 2 fifths of wine at least once last month**	4
Drank 8 shots at least once last month*	12

*Approximately 5 ounces of pure ethanol.
**Approximately 6 ounces of pure ethanol.
Median time to drink: 5 hours.

large quantities of alcohol. The consumption of five ounces of pure ethanol over a period of five hours by a 160-pound person would result in a Blood Alcohol Content (BAC) of approximately 0.23 per cent. A BAC of 0.10 per cent is considered legally drunk in 48 states and a BAC of 0.23 per cent would take approximately six or seven hours to metabolise down to 0.10 per cent.

Problems Associated with Drinking

Table 7.10 shows the self-reported problems resulting from alcohol use in the past year. The numbers speak for themselves and indicate a serious need for services among the railroad population. These percentages refer to a population size of 234,000.

It can be seen that in the past year one-third of those who are married have had a spouse get upset over the respondent's drinking. One-sixth have had a serious argument because of it. Furthermore, data not shown in the tables indicates that in their lifetimes, one in twelve has seen his home life deteriorate because of drinking and one out of 50 has had his marriage break up because of drinking.

The most serious consequences at work are absenteeism and inability to perform properly ('half man') with prevalences of eight and four per cent, respectively. The 'life in general' sections raise even more concern. After drinking, two per cent have had automobile accidents in the past year, and three per cent have been involved in fist fights. One per cent of railroad workers on the railroads studied have been arrested by the police as a consequence of drinking in the past year.

Table 7.10: Problems Associated with Drinking in the Past Year

	Percentage
Home life	
Spouse upset*	33
Serious arguments with spouse*	18
Hit spouse*	2
Hit children**	1
Work life	
Boss upset	2
Self injury	0.4
Other injury	0.1
Serious argument	2
Absent	8
Half man	4
Suspended	0.4
Fight with customer	0.2
Life in general	
Fist fight	3
Auto accident	2
Arrested	1

*Based upon those currently married.
**Based upon those respondents currently living with their children.

Conclusion

These analyses demonstrate that many railroad workers have problems related to drinking. Such problems have serious potential consequences for the workers, their families, their employers and the public.

Many of America's railroads, the railroad labour organisations, and the federal government have recognised this problem for many years, although this is the first quantitative study of the phenomenon. The first railroad employee assistance program was established in 1951, making it one of the oldest programs in any industry in the country.

The data being reported here are not the results of idle scientific curiosity. They are part of an *action* research program. On the basis of these results and of an evaluation of the methods and successes of employee assistance programs in the railroad, as well as other industries, recommendations are being made both for the improvement of present employee assistance programs and for the establishment of effective new programs in the industry. Hopefully, if this study is replicated ten years from now, lower numbers will be reported.

PART THREE

THE INDUSTRIAL RESPONSE

INTRODUCTION

Brian D. Hore

The remaining section of this book deals with types of industrial response to the theoretical and actual problems arising from alcohol use. A wide range of views spanning continents is described, even though there may be major industrial differences between countries. In essence however it would seem that the industrial response falls into two broad areas: first, the area of prevention in which industry takes on the role of attempting to prevent alcohol-related problems occurring and secondly, the differing systems of case identification in which employees with alcohol-related problems are identified and subsequently dealt with. In some countries it would seem that there is much greater emphasis on the latter than the former.

Prevention

This includes both general education of the workforce about the potential problems that excessive drinking can cause and also informing workers of the industrial risks from alcohol use. This will also include an awareness of the high risks in certain occupational groups within industry. Such measures as restriction of alcohol at the workplace, and the provision of alternative beverages to alcohol are also important in prevention. In these ways industry is not only increasing the education of its employees but also taking responsibility, so that employees will not be put at special risk in developing alcohol abuse or alcohol-related problems.

Case Identification

Case identification and subsequent management seem to show broad similarity in several countries. It seems clear that before any such system can be introduced there has to be a union/management negotiation and support both at plant level and higher level in both organisations. It would also seem agreed that identification by a *reduction of work performance* is the most widely-used criterion,

131

although in some countries, e.g. France, with a regular system of medical examination of all employees, other methods to increase detection are available. It also seems agreed that there should be either a written company policy or, at the very least, a clear understanding of the response of industry to individuals with alcohol-related problems with a clear specification of differing responsibilities in producing that industrial response. Clearly there are differences in who is to do what, e.g. what sort of individual would be the co-ordinator and organiser of such programs. Similar differences may occur in relation to the method of counselling once it is decided that a reduction in work performance or some other measurement has indicated alcohol-related problems due to drinking. Some take the view that this whole process is basically one in which discipline is deferred, i.e. the individual is still under disciplinary procedures which are just being obviated providing the subject takes treatment. In other cases it seems the situation is not regarded in any way as a disciplinary one but as 'sickness'.

It is variably argued that people responsible for such programs should have an industrial background or an alcoholism background or a medical or personnel background. It does seem agreed that deterioration of work performance will present cases at an earlier stage which should result in improved treatment.

Clearly the majority of endeavour is in these areas of education and case identification with perhaps little done for those who have been rendered unemployed by their alcohol problem. However, in one country, Norway, there are encouraging reports of work programs based on a behavioural model which have been implemented in relation to young and unemployed alcoholics or drug addicts with disturbed backgrounds.

In many countries, e.g. the UK, such programs seem largely absent. Indeed in the UK regrettably, apart from a handful of industrial programs in relation to case identification and referral, there appears to be little done either in terms of education or attempting to re-employ those with alcohol-related problems who have become unemployed. It is hoped that legislation in relation to the health and safety at work act will increase the educational component of such programs and that wider interest will be taken both by management and unions in relation to case detection, and referral placement. It is also to be hoped even if only in a pilot way, that some attention is paid to the Norwegian model, as finding employment or retraining individuals who have had long periods of unemployment due to alcohol-related disorders proves frequently a major problem in clinical practice.

8 ONE COMPANY'S EXPERIENCE

Allan F. Blacklaws

By virtue of the commodity which they produce, brewery companies have a particularly high proportion of workers with alcohol-related problems. It is not really surprising to find that on occasion the consumption of beer — so readily available in vast quantities, albeit unofficially — gives rise to problems of discipline, absenteeism, illness and poor performance.

Some years ago as part of a comprehensive program of reviewing existing personnel policies and formulating new ones, Scottish & Newcastle Breweries Limited (S & NB) recognised that a social problem of some magnitude existed and that some action was necessary to safeguard the health of its employees and the reputation of the company. The first step was to accept that alcohol problems should be regarded constructively and can often be overcome. The second was to recognise that by the nature of the drink trade, employees were exposed to a greater risk of developing alcohol-related problems than people in many other industries. The third step was to admit that despite the fact that the company depended for its existence on the manufacture and sale of alcohol, excessive or inappropriate drinking sometimes causes problems.

It was from these small beginnings that the company developed its present progressive policy on drink and its related problems. We were much assisted by evidence that family, and other social factors, are often major influences on drinking habits and alcohol-related problems. In particular we were influenced by recent evidence that individuals working in a 'high-risk' industry such as brewing are especially likely to become heavy drinkers and to experience alcohol-related problems (Murray, 1975; Plant, 1979a). On the positive side it was judged to be encouraging that many employees who were guilty of drinking too much could be helped either to abstain or to reduce their alcohol consumption to an acceptable, harmless level (Schramm, 1977).

Between 1975 and 1978 S & NB employees took part in a research project which confirmed that many people applying for jobs in the licensed trade were already fairly heavy drinkers and considered 'normal drinking' to be far in excess of the standard accepted by people entering other occupations (Plant, 1979a). It subsequently transpired that most of the people from the drink-trade group had increased their alcohol consumption by considerable amounts after having been in the industry for three years or so, and the number of problems this created was correspondingly high.

As noted in Chapter 2, this study showed that the drink-trade workers experienced exceptionally high rates of alcohol-related problems such as stomach ulcers, drunkenness arrests and difficulties at work. Reassuringly, it was also shown that some alcohol-related problems were only temporary. Some men were so worried by their drinking habits and the effects of these on both family and working life that they had given up their jobs in the drink trade and had sought 'drier', safer work elsewhere. As a result of this their drinking habits had changed dramatically for the better. We felt we ought to be able to provide a climate where the habit was not formed in the first instance and, if we failed in this objective, there should be some mechanism whereby the job, and therefore the household income, was safeguarded. This could only be achieved by a rehabilitation program.

The size of the problem was intimidating. S & NB employ approximately 27,000 people in locations as far apart as Lerwick in the Shetland Isles to Southampton in Hampshire. The company distills whisky on the Isle of Jura and on Speyside, brews ale and lager in Edinburgh, Newcastle and Manchester, and bottles spirits in Leith and wines at Felling. Its public houses and hotels, spread throughout the country, sell a wide range of alcoholic beverages most of which are consumed on the premises. Employees are thus in frequent contact with liquor.

There is strict security at all stages of alcohol production and sales. In addition, there are recognised procedures to ensure that individuals caught stealing alcohol are disciplined. Even so, human nature is such that the tighter the surveillance, the greater is the challenge to beat the system, especially when success is enjoyable. Such activities gain further support from the widespread belief that taking beer from a brewery is not really stealing anyway. Salesmen are in daily touch with the product as are members of the many delivery fleets and the team of people who service the dispensing equipment in bars. Even the administrative and managerial staff are not immune because they are usually located in premises close to where the product is manufactured or packaged, distributed or sold. While most employees manage to cope with their work situation, the availability of alcohol does lead to problems for some.

The responsibility of a public company in the latter part of the twentieth century is much greater than simply paying wages for work done. There is a greater awareness by management of the pressures which beset a workforce. Some of the problems in the industrial relations field have arisen because companies have become too big and impersonal. In order to simplify work methods and encourage greater productivity the very soul of job satisfaction has been destroyed and people feel that they have become human machines instead of human beings. This has led to problems involving relationships, including the challenge to authority and the fear of change in a flexible environment. ·

There are corresponding problems beyond the work situation, exemplified by the rise in cases of delinquency, vandalism and football hooliganism. It is generally accepted that alcohol misuse is a major factor contributing to these problems.

One of the delightful characteristics of the British working man is his loyalty to his colleagues, even though there are occasions when this is misguided. One facet of this is the way people cover up for friends and workmates who are really in need of assistance. In a workshop or office, colleagues will make all manner of excuses for people who are missing or not performing well, especially at the beginning or the end of the working week. Managers and supervisors will look with suspicion at yet another sick note referring to a stomach disorder; but they tend to accept these at face value, partly because they are too busy with their production targets to find time to fully investigate them. In a rare case they may even be sympathetic because they themselves have to cope with similar personal problems. Managers are often not very perceptive in relation to this issue. The following report by a senior executive exemplifies this:

At first, when Mr X admitted that he was an alcoholic I was very surprised. I knew that he had been a fairly heavy and steady drinker for years and heard of the odd occasion when he hadn't arrived home until two o'clock in the morning very drunk. But an alcoholic? Impossible. Then I thought back over a year, a number of accidents, seemingly innocent and acceptable or explainable at the time, came to mind. I realised that Mr X's work performance had deteriorated. His reports had been late for successive months. There had also been a number of careless mistakes for which there was no real and acceptable explanation. Going further back I

recalled that, on perhaps five or six occasions Mr X had been off due
to 'an upset stomach'. There had been several days when he was
late due to 'not feeling well', 'the car not starting' or 'the dog
running away'.

As I write this I begin to wonder how on earth I failed to recognise
the symptoms of a serious drinking problem. Yet these different
incidents did not seem to relate to each other.

With the wisdom of hindsight other 'signs' come to mind. These
include:

> failing to deputise for me at a meeting when I was in London;
> telling me he was in one place when he was somewhere else;
> being shut out of his house by his wife because he was 'in such
> a state';
> his recent association with another employee who was also a
> very heavy drinker, and who had been recently 'demoted';
> seldom being able to get him on the telephone in the evenings or
> at the weekends.

I suppose that I could add to this list but these illustrations will,
I think, serve to indicate the areas where perhaps I should have
looked more closely. And yet, so many of them were happening
outside office hours and were not really my concern as his manager:
or were they?

Mr X and I have always had a good working relationship. The fact
that he confided in me completely proves that the relationship still
exists. The fact that he was able to hide the situation from me for
so long I would put down to his 'ability to survive' as much as to
my 'lack of recognition' but in my heart of hearts I know I should
have noticed.

The policy which allowed this sympathetic approach to be taken was
not developed overnight. It progressed gradually with consultations
taking place with bodies like the Scottish Health Education Unit and
the Scottish Council on Alcoholism. The trade unions with whom we
negotiate were involved from the early days. Our overall approach has
four separate strands:

(1) to donate money to agencies responsibile for the treatment of
    problem drinkers;
(2) to make facilities available to bodies undertaking research
    projects;
(3) actively to discourage drinking on company premises;
(4) to offer a counselling service to our employees.

The company accepts that it has a social responsibility to give financial aid to several councils on alcoholism in areas where there are large numbers of its employees. This has the additional advantage of strengthening counselling and treatment services which may be used by employees who require such help. Other British drink-trade organisations regularly make similar financial contributions to treatment and research.

Trade union support and involvement is vital to the success of establishing a company alcoholism policy. Because of this the chairman of S & NB, together with the Scottish Regional Secretary of the Transport & General Workers Union, convened a meeting of the leaders of industry and the trade union movement in Scotland. Not only did this bring together the parties most concerned but it also provided an opportunity for a joint program of action to be debated. As the spokesman for the trade union movement said:

Someone who is not capable due to alcohol is a danger to other workers . . . there is also the question of dealing with his social and domestic life . . . many homes have been broken up . . . we have lost quite a few of our members . . . an alcoholic shop-floor worker is often treated differently from an alcoholic who is a member of management where it can be hidden . . . prolonged sickness allowed . . . and a golden handshake . . . with the shop-floor worker, it is often too late to do something and he has to be dismissed.

In the area of research it is sometimes difficult for students to gain access to records and to obtain contact with employees, so S & NB have co-operated in studies of this kind, usually the time spent has been valuable. But the main thrusts of our policy are in reducing drinking at work and on personal counselling of those with problems.

Until relatively recently it was traditional in breweries to supply employees with what in Scotland was called 'pundy'. This was an allocation of beer — about two pints per day — to which every adult employee was entitled provided it was consumed on the premises. It was perhaps acceptable for non-drivers in summer for, by their very nature, some jobs involve hard physical labour. Delivering several tons of kegs each weighing 1.5 cwt to public houses is no easy task. Clearing spent grains from large vessels and working with barley in malt-kilns is hot, sweaty work and a drink of beer can be most refreshing. But in winter the situation is different. Imagine the position of large numbers of workers employed in an open-ended shed cleaning casks and at the appropriate time queuing up with their pint mugs, and sometimes dried-milk cans, to draw their allocation of beer on cold, wet mornings; or picture the scene on another occasion in a transport bothy when the then new personnel manager was addressing some 200 draymen at 7.30 a.m. on a damp, foggy November morning with the men each having a pint mug in their hands before going off in their vehicles to make deliveries. Much better and more civilised is the modern practice which enables employees to draw an allowance of canned beer from their local public houses and take it home for consumption there.

The outlines of the company's policy on drinking problems at work are as follows:

(1) The company recognises, from the nature of its business, that employees can be exposed to greater risks of problem drinking than in other types of industry.

(2) It acknowledges that alcoholism is an illness characterised by dependence on alcohol, either psychological or physical, or a combination of both. In the industrial context, it is defined as drinking which continually or repeatedly affects the work performance of the employee.

(3) The most important signs of this can be detected by managers as:
  — frequent lateness
  — repeated brief periods of absence
  — minor accidents on the job
  — drinking at work
  — changes of mood
  — borrowing money
  — lowering quality of work
  — reduced quantity of output
  — medical certificates for absence will frequently include diagnoses like gastro-enteritis, dyspepsia, nervous debility and so on.

(4) On recognition of a problem or potential problem, the manager will seek the advice of the personnel and medical departments who have the necessary professional contacts to start the treatment process.

(5) The individual will be encouraged to seek help and treatment on the understanding that:
  (a) He or she whilst undergoing treatment will be considered to

be on sick leave and will be entitled to the normal benefits
from the appropriate company sickness benefit scheme.
(b) His or her position will be made available upon return to
work following treatment, unless it is mutually agreed that
a change would be desirable and beneficial.
(c) No disciplinary action will be taken against the employee
unless it is clear that the individual is incapable of respond-
ing to treatment or refuses the advice and guidance which
has been given by the professional advisers invited to deal
with the case.
(d) Any individual who has offended the disciplinary code
and who claims that he or she does not require treatment
will be warned under the normal procedures concerned
with behaviour and work performance.
(6) This policy is applicable to all employees from directors to
wage earners and there will be no discrimination at any level.
(Blacklaws, 1978)

It can be seen from the foregoing that the whole basis of the counselling
process lies in the definition of drinking as something which affects
work performance and the cure is a combination of our sickness and
disciplinary systems.

The crucial question at this stage is 'does it work?' And the answer
is, 'only sometimes'. Here are extracts from some reports prepared by
personnel managers:

The first case involved an employee who was obviously verging on
the chronic. An interview was arranged with an official of the local
council on alcoholism but he was not convinced that he had a drinking
problem and was not interested in attending therapy sessions. He was
informed that any further breach of discipline would result in his
dismissal and the inevitable happened. He is no longer employed by
the company.

The second case concerns a tradesman who was single and lived
with his mother until her death. The public house was the centre of his
social life and when left on his own he became depressed and his
alcohol consumption increased. His work performance deteriorated
and his attendance became poor. At first he was reluctant to admit
that he was an alcoholic, but he eventually agreed to attend an
alcoholism unit at the local psychiatric hospital. Further trouble
ensued and he had to be dried out after an emergency admission.
When he had sufficiently recovered he was persuaded to move from

his job to a new department where he could make a fresh start. During that period he was supported by the company medical department and group therapy sessions. He developed an interest in voluntary work with old people, has remained abstinent, and has returned to his old job where he is working well.

In the third case the employee not only freely admitted that he was seriously addicted to alcohol, but was extremely relieved to discuss this with his manager and responded eagerly to the suggestion of treatment. He remained sober for a few months, but then regrettably disappeared from work and home for days on end. This process was repeated and he was dismissed eventually as no prolonged progress was being made.

The fourth case is about a manager who had been warned previously that he might have a drink problem. He had discussions with his personnel manager but refused to reduce his intake. A follow-up interview was arranged but he did not attend. The next contact came when he lost his driving licence due to a drunken-driving charge and he was transferred to a temporary job. During this time he was referred to an alcoholism unit where supportive treatment in the field of interpersonal relationships was recommended. The medical department helped with this and he has now remained sober for some time. He will be reassessed in a few months. If progress remains satisfactory there is every possibility of his returning to his former post which involves driving a company car.

These cases illustrate the opportunities and frustrations of dealing with human problems in an understanding fashion. The constructive approach adopted under the S & NB policy is one of the first of its type implemented in Britain. Most of the individual cases dealt with since the policy's inception have not been documented. This is because the company decided that such records might undermine the perceived confidentiality that has been vital to establishing the new policy. While this decision was reached on practical grounds, it has clearly precluded a formal evaluation of the effectiveness of the policy. So far very few British companies have initiated such constructive policies to manage alcohol problems and there have so far been no detailed evaluations of the type produced in other countries, notably the United States (e.g. Schramm, Mandell and Archer, 1978). In spite of the absence of a complete and detailed evaluation those involved in operating the S & NB policy report that successes outnumber failures. They further conclude that at present only the surface of the total problem with the workforce is being scratched.

It is important to realise that having a policy does not necessarily change attitudes nor improve things by itself. These only come by managers and those with a drinking problem working together with a great deal of understanding and sincerity and a deep knowledge that confidentiality will be observed and security of employment assured.

In the case of S & NB there is still much to be achieved, particularly in the field of education. We have just commissioned a consultancy company to prepare a communication package which will make our employees at all levels more aware of the facts about alcohol problems and of the company's policy on such problems at work. This will take the form of an audio-visual program supplemented by two booklets. The film-strip program will present information in a matter-of-fact manner and will publicise the effects of alcohol on physical and mental behaviour. It will cover both social and excessive drinking and will show the effects of drinking on performance at work. It will be coupled with an outline of the company procedure for dealing with employees who suffer from drink-related problems.

The first booklet will be for employees and will contain a summary of the script with a reproduction of some of the pictures and these will act as an *aide memoire*: it will also contain some additional facts and figures about alcohol, e.g. the effect of different drinks on blood/ alcohol levels and on physical and mental performance, and the effect of evening drinking on top of lunch-time drinking and what alcohol does on 'the morning after the night before'.

The second booklet will be for managers and will contain all the information from the employees' booklet together with practical information which will act as a guide to action. This will specify the procedure to be followed in cases or suspected cases of drink-related problems amongst subordinates and colleagues and will be illustrated with case histories.

It is a sad fact that after years of recognition of the dangers of excessive drinking, we believe that managers, shop stewards and employees generally still require a deeper knowledge of this subject. They need training on how to identify the patterns of behaviour which might indicate that a problem exists and of the steps to be taken to implement our written policies. We feel that all our people must be encouraged to provide the kind of support necessary to carry through the program in a spirit of understanding. And we despair at the time it takes to inch forward. But when we are weary and depressed we turn again to an article which appeared in our works newspaper in the following terms:

Don't be ashamed to admit you're an alcoholic — and stop worrying about your job. These are two pieces of advice I gladly offer to anyone who is privately worrying about what most people politely describe as 'a drink problem'. I know, for I've been through an emotional mill that left me a bit bruised but happier and healthier than I had been for years . . . Fortunately — for me — I reached a personal crisis which led me to seek medical advice. When I look back now it seems incredibly simple and I wonder why I was so nervous about approaching my doctor, my boss and my friends and asking them 'please help me'. (Anonymous, 1977a)

If there is one thing I've learned over this whole sad saga it is that people do care when their workmates hit a problem. And if you are honest with them and ask them to help you the outcome is totally surprising in the pleasantest way. (Anonymous, 1977b)

As this chapter describes, S & NB now have a constructive policy for helping employees with drinking problems that affect their work. This policy is still in its infancy. Conclusions so far can only be tentative. Even so, it is apparent that the majority of employees who develop conspicuous drinking problems can be helped to overcome these, at least in relation to their work performance. And that must be good for them, for us, and for society.

9 POLICIES IN THE UNITED STATES

William S. Dunkin

Background

Employee alcoholism programs are not a new phenomenon in the
United States. Their history goes back to 1942, when the first such
program was started at E.I. du Pont de Nemours and Company in
Wilmington, Delaware.

This early program, and a number of others which followed in the
next few years, dealt only with those individuals whose drinking had
become such an obvious and obnoxious problem that it was common
knowledge. Despite the fact that there were few specialised alcoholism
treatment facilities available in those days, the du Pont program (and
others) consistently achieved long-term, stable recoveries in at least
two-thirds of all cases. This was during a period when the most
successful treatment facilities in the country considered themselves
fortunate if they achieved a 20 per cent recovery rate.

Some of these early programs reasoned, quite correctly, that their
supervisors (at all levels) were the ideal vehicle for 'spotting'
alcoholics and referring them to the program. They, therefore, trained
their supervisors to do this. Unfortunately the training was based
upon two erroneous assumptions.

First, they assumed that the 'alcoholic' was *readily identifiable* by
the supervisor through observation of the physical and behavioural
symptoms associated with the popular stereotype, i.e. bloodshot eyes,
shaking hands, frequent trips to the water cooler in the morning,
constant use of breath sweeteners, loud and obnoxious conduct, lack
of cleanliness and personal grooming, etc. Secondly, they assumed
that any employee not displaying such readily-identifiable signs
could not be an alcoholic, and therefore need not be referred to
the program.

A number of programs are still in existence which operate on this
conceptual approach. Unfortunately, this means that only those
employees who exhibit the most extreme forms of alcohol-related
harm receive help. This approach obviously misses the large majority
of employees who are impaired, but to a lesser degree, by alcohol
misuse and this means, additionally, that the employer misses out on
the economic benefits and personnel rewards obtainable through an

144

effective employee alcoholism program.

Role of the National Council on Alcoholism

In the early 1960s, the National Council on Alcoholism, the only national voluntary, non-profit health agency in the alcoholism field, made an extensive survey, covering more than 72,000 employees in large, multi-plant industries throughout the United States. This survey was made to determine the prevalence of alcoholism in industry, but it also discovered the basic principle which underlies the modern approach to the problem of employee alcoholism.

This principle, simply stated, is that any problem drinker, even on suffering the less extreme alcohol-related disabilities, will exhibit a pattern of deteriorating and/or substandard job performance which can be observed quite readily by the supervisor literally years (five to ten on the average) before the more serious, chronic types of alcohol-related harm become visible.

This led to a new approach in which referrals to the program were based on unsatisfactory job performance, but, in many cases, the supervisors were told to initiate referral procedures only when they 'suspected' that the unsatisfactory performance was due to the individual's drinking. The following language (in a book of instructions to supervisors) is typical of programs using this approach, which is a 'misguided merger' of the techniques of the early 1940s with the knowledge gained two decades later.

> The supervisor is not expected to make a diagnosis of alcoholism. Corrective interviews and referrals will be based strictly on documented instances of unsatisfactory performance, violations of work rules, and other strictly objective criteria . . . When the supervisor has reason to believe (or suspects) that the unsatisfactory job performance is due to alcoholism, the employee should be referred to the medical department.

Unfortunately the second sentence virtually wipes out the advantage of the job performance approach, since it restricts all corrective action and referral *only* to those employees whom the supervisor can 'identify' as alcoholics, and the net result is a return to the outmoded approach of the 1940s.

Successful Techniques

The approach being used in all successful programs today is one in which supervisors are called upon to do exactly what they are being paid to do — monitor job performance and conduct corrective interviews where indicated. The only difference that the existence of the program creates for the supervisor is that it offers a comfortable tool to be used in the corrective interviews — a constructive offer of confidential help (diagnosis, counselling, treatment, whatever may be needed) for any problem which might be causing the poor job performance. If continued poor performance requires disciplinary action, then the supervisor may offer referral to the program as an alternative to that discipline — up to, and including, termination.

This approach solves what has been one of the most persistent problems of employee alcoholism programs — the unfortunate practice of getting management involved in the diagnostic and treatment functions which should be solely the business of qualified medical and paramedical professionals.

The application of this new approach brought about some startling results. The NCA survey had calculated the prevalence of alcoholism in industry at between four per cent and ten per cent of any employed population and the cost thereof was set at one-quarter of the alcoholic employee's annual wages. Both figures have since been shown to be extremely conservative. Present day estimates are five per cent to ten per cent, with six per cent figured as the usual minimum, and many programs have reported cost savings of one-quarter of alcoholic employees' wages in *reduced absenteeism alone*.

Where formerly programs had reached only a tiny fraction of these estimated alcoholic populations, the new approach in some cases reached 15 per cent to 20 per cent per year. Furthermore, it was demonstrated that problem drinkers who were reached before their degree of impairment was extreme were more likely to achieve long-term, stable recoveries, so 'success rates' went even higher than before.

NCA's labour-management consultants warned employers that the surest way to guarantee failure of a program was even to allow the supervisors to 'look for alcoholics'. Referrals to the program were to be based strictly on poor job performance. This brought about two basic changes in programs.

First, the program had to have a title which was *non-diagnostic* — something such as 'Employee Counselling Service', 'Employee

Assistance Program', or the like. This was because there are a number
of other personal and/or medical problems which can and do affect job
performance adversely. Referral to an 'alcoholism' program would
obviously be contra-indicated in these cases. Employers saw resolution
of these other problems for their employees as a 'fringe benefit' of such
a program since these employees, too, could be restored to happy,
productive lives.

However, employers were told — and results of successful programs
showed it to be a fact — that most of the individuals who were referred
on the basis of poor job performance were in that group because of
their drinking. The average percentage is 65 per cent to 70 per cent
and, in some cases, it runs higher in the early years of the program.
But the problem of alcoholism is greater than *all other problems
combined*.

This meant that the program had to have an expert on alcoholism
and alcoholics at the point of referral — someone capable of ruling in
or ruling out drinking as the cause of the poor job performance. Often
this individual was a recovered alcoholic or a non-alcoholic who had
had long experience in dealing with alcoholics in a one-to-one situation.

Secondly basic treatment of alcoholism (or of any other problem
encountered) took place *outside* the workplace, just as it would for
any other illness. The employee alcoholism program recommended by
NCA is a 'pre-treatment' program of early identification and motivation
of the alcoholic to accept treatment.

Role of the Union

Also discovered in the 1960s by NCA was the key role which unions
could play in these 'pre-treatment' programs. Far-sighted union
leaders who learned of the job-performance approach to the problem
of employee alcoholism realised that their traditional position of saying,
'We will fight to save your job no matter what it costs!' was no longer
valid when the *life of the union member was one of those costs*.

The partnership of labour and management in a totally co-ordinated
effort to achieve their mutual objectives is vital to the success of any
job-based alcoholism program. Labour, because of its relationship
with its members, can give understanding and a sympathetic offer of
assistance, counselling, and treatment. Yet there is overwhelming
evidence that alcoholics rarely respond favourably to this approach.

Management has an effective approach through its legitimate right to initiate corrective action when the employee's job performance falls below minimum accepted standards. At this point, maximum motivation can be achieved by giving the employee a firm, fair choice between accepting confidential help or accepting the disciplinary consequences of the poor job performance.

The general functions of management and labour, respectively, in an effective 'pre-treatment' program will now be listed.

Management Functions

These might be:

(1) To create a company-wide climate by all available means, including employee education, which will gradually eliminate the effects of the social stigma associated with alcoholism, which acts as a barrier to constructive corrective action.
(2) To enlist the joint partnership to labour in initiating and implementing the 'pre-treatment' program.
(3) To bring the full capabilities of the supervisory staff, from top management to front-line foremen, to bear on the early identification and motivation to treatment of any employee whose job-performance deficiencies do not respond to normal corrective procedures.
(4) To assign clear-cut responsibility to all levels of supervision and labour leadership in the implementation of pre-treatment procedures and to develop a positive program of follow-up to assure that such procedures are consistently followed on a continuous basis.
(5) To schedule initial and follow-up orientation and training meetings for all supervisory personnel (including top management), labour leaders, front-line foremen, and other labour representatives.
(6) To maintain adequate, continuing written records covering day-to-day patterns of absence, unsatisfactory work performance, formal and informal disciplinary actions taken, and any other relevant data that indicate developing employee problems.

Union Functions

Union functions in the pre-treatment program are entirely consistent with traditional functions of shop stewards and other union representatives. In implementing the agreed-upon policy and procedures, the unions will represent their members' interest by assuring that:

(1) The employee's job security and promotional opportunities are not jeopardised by a request for diagnosis and treatment.
(2) The focus of corrective interviews is restricted to the issue of job performance rather than judgements on alcoholism (unless a violation of work rules against drinking on the job is involved).
(3) The confidential nature of all medical and program records is preserved.
(4) Any employee who has drinking problems will receive the same careful consideration and offer of treatment extended to employees who have any illness.
(5) All other rights and privileges inherent in the agreed-upon policy and procedures are protected.

Shop stewards and supervisors working as a team to motivate employees to accept needed treatment should significantly reduce alcohol-related grievances. Indeed, we have evidence in one such program (Oldsmobile) that there was a reduction of 78 per cent in the number of grievances filed by the alcoholics who had gone through that program (Labour-Management Alcoholism Journal, 1974a). Shop stewards are also in an excellent position to encourage the earliest possible use of union counselling services for members with problems and to stimulate self-referrals for treatment.

Program Implementation

The implementation of an effective employee alcoholism program requires little expense and the program itself can be easily integrated into existing management procedures with regard to job performance and disciplinary actions.

A written policy on alcoholism is not only an essential first step in developing an effective employee alcoholism program, but is, in fact, the foundation upon which the entire program must be built. In any organised company, such a policy should be developed jointly between management and the union leadership and should be signed by the chief executive officer of the firm and the president of the union. The reason why such a policy is necessary when dealing with alcohol-related problems (employers do not have policies on heart disease, cancer, or the like) is the stigma which surrounds such problems.

Every organisation which does not have a written policy on

alcoholism is forced to operate with an 'unwritten policy', which is
well-known to all employees, particularly any of them who may have
a drinking problem. If put into typical corporate language this unwritten policy might read:

> Any employee who can successfully conceal his/her alcoholism
> from management will be entitled to all privileges and benefits of
> this company, including paid sick leave, vacations, regular raises,
> promotions, etc. When the employee can no longer conceal the
> alcoholism, termination will result.

The acceptance and credibility of the employee alcoholism program
will depend upon how well its written policy provides clear-cut
answers to questions which are uppermost in the minds of the affected
(alcoholic) employees. Some of the crucial questions which must be
answered by management (and jointly by unions and management in
an organised workforce) are:

(1) Does the organisation really accept that alcohol-related problems
warrant a constructive approach?
(2) How are alcohol-related problems defined for program purposes?
(3) Will alcohol-related problems be handled sympathetically?
(4) Will a request for or acceptance of treatment affect job
security or promotional opportunities?
(5) Will program records be kept in strict confidence?
(6) What are the consequences of refusing or failing to respond to
treatment?
(7) Will there be opportunity for self-referral on a confidential
basis.
(8) Is the primary purpose to encourage employees to seek diagnosis
and treatment in order to arrest problem drinking as early as
possible?

Many employers have employee benefit programs covering a wide range
of behavioural/medical and other problems, and have developed
written policies which include alcoholism in the total list of problems
covered. There is nothing wrong with this in theory. However,
experience has shown that employee alcoholism programs achieve their
maximum potential in terms of early identification and motivation to
accept treatment *only when the alcoholism program has its own highly-
visible identity* and when answers to questions which are crucial to

employees and their families are provided either in a separate policy or statement of position, which can be communicated effectively to all employees and their families.

The joint policy statement which follows has been approved by leaders of organised labour in the United States as well as by members of top management of some of the most prestigious industries in that country.

(1) Alcoholism is recognised as a disease for which there is effective treatment and rehabilitation.

(2) Alcoholism is defined as a disease in which a person's consumption of any alcoholic beverage definitely and repeatedly interferes with that individual's health and/or job performance.

(3) Persons who suspect that they may have an alcoholism problem, even in its early stages, are encouraged to seek diagnosis and to follow through with the treatment that may be prescribed by qualified professionals, in order to arrest the disease as early as possible.

(4) Any persons having this disease will receive the same careful consideration and offer of treatment that is presently extended, under existing benefit plans, to all those having any other disease.

(5) The same benefits and insurance coverages that are provided for all other diseases, under established benefit plans, will be available for individuals who accept medically-approved treatment for alcoholism.

(6) This policy is not concerned with social drinking, but rather with the disease of alcoholism. The concern is limited to those instances of alcoholism which affect the job performance of the individual. The policy is designed solely to achieve restoration of health and full recovery.

(7) It will be the responsibility of all management and union personnel to implement this policy and to follow the procedures which have been designed to assure that no person with alcoholism will have either job security or promotional opportunities jeopardised by a request for diagnosis and treatment.

(8) Neither supervisors nor union representatives have the qualifications to diagnose alcoholism as a disease. Therefore, referral for diagnosis and treatment will be based on job performance, within the terms, conditions, and application of the union-management agreement.

(9) The decision to request diagnosis and accept treatment for

alcoholism is the personal responsibility of the individual.

(10) An individual's refusal to accept referral for diagnosis or to follow prescribed treatment will be handled in accordance with existing contractual agreements and union-management understandings with respect to job performance.

(11) The confidential nature of the medical records of individuals with alcoholism will be strictly preserved.

(12) Persons participating in this program will be expected to meet existing job performance standards and established work rules within the framework of existing union-management agreements. Any exceptions to this requirement will be by mutual agreement between the union and management.

(13) Nothing in this statement of policy is to be interpreted as constituting a waiver of management's responsibility to maintain discipline or the right to take disciplinary measures, within the framework of the collective bargaining agreement, in the case of misconduct that may result from alcoholism (National Council on Alcoholism, 1976).

Program Definition

The program itself can be defined as the mechanism for implementing the organisation's policy. It follows that the second logical and essential step is the development of specific procedures which must be followed by all levels of supervision to accomplish this.

In most organisations this is done by setting up a joint union-management committee. This should be composed of equal representation from both groups. It should include (as co-chairman) a top-ranking management executive with authority to establish and implement policy on behalf of the company and a counterpart or counterparts with equivalent authority in the union(s).

This committee will have a number of functions, the first of which should be to develop the specific procedures to be followed by all management and union supervisory personnel in order to implement the agreed-upon written policy.

Other functions should include, but need not be limited to, the following:

(1) To specify and assure the development of a training program for all supervisors and union respresentatives.

(2) To determine the personnel, materials, equipment, and budget needed to initiate the program.

(3) To assist in solving problems that may develop in the implementation of the program.

(4) To develop confidential record-keeping systems which may be needed to assure evaluation of program effectiveness.

(5) To monitor all aspects of program progress and effectiveness.

(6) To develop ideas or activities which might increase program effectiveness, particularly in the areas of prevention and education.

(7) To keep abreast of new developments, techniques, resources, and referral agencies.

(8) To assist in developing a list of and evaluating the alcoholism services in the community.

(9) To assure that group health benefits cover alcoholism for persons who accept treatment.

(10) To select a program administrator to provide staff services to the committee and to be responsible for implementing the committee's decisions as well as performing the tasks assigned by it.

Suggested Procedures

Individual cases either originate through voluntary referral or are referred on the basis of a job performance interview with the supervisor and the union representative, if desired. In the latter type of case, the following procedures are suggested:

(1) The focus of the first interview should be restricted to the issue of job performance. Opinions or judgements on alcoholism should be avoided.

(2) The employee should have the right to have a union representative present at the interview.

(3) After the job performance has been reviewed by the supervisor and the union representative, if desired, the employee should be informed on an absolutely confidential basis of the professional services available, including diagnosis and counselling.

(4) The employee may choose to accept or reject the offer of confidential help and services. If the employee chooses to accept, referral should be made directly to a qualified professional

counselling and diagnostic facility that has been approved by
the committee, for a determination as to whether or not the
problem is alcoholism.

(5) If the employee rejects the offer, and the job performance
problems do not recur after the interview, there is no longer a
problem.

(6) If the job performance problems recur, then the union representative and the supervisor may agree that the employee's performance is not acceptable and the next appropriate step is to
offer the employee a firm choice between accepting the
assistance offered by the program or accepting whatever action
is appropriate within the framework of existing union-
management agreements.

(7) In the majority of cases, when confronted with this clear-cut
choice, the employee will choose to use the services of the
program and thus may be referred directly to the committee-
approved resource as in section (4) above to determine whether
or not the problem is alcoholism.

(8) If the employee still refuses the offer of help, then appropriate
action should be taken within the framework of existing union-
management agreements.

(9) Referral to a qualified diagnostic service may result in one of
two types of conclusion with differing end results, as follows:

  (a) The employee is suffering from alcoholism, or the
       problem is alcohol-related.

  (b) The employee is not suffering from alcoholism, or the
       problem is not alcohol-related.

In case (a), the employee should be referred to appropriate alcoholism
treatment in committee-approved facilities or resources. In case (b), the
employee should be referred to the indicated union counselling
facility or other community resource approved by the joint committee
(Labour-Management Alcoholism Journal, 1974a).

Secondary Prevention

In the United States today, there is an effective, tested method of
achieving secondary prevention of alcoholism on a broad scale through
the joint efforts of unions and employer organisations who initiate
and implement pre-treatment programs of early identification and

motivation to accept treatment for those employees who suffer from the disease. The success of any secondary prevention effort is directly proportionate to the time elapsing between the onset of the disease, and the time it is detected and the patient is motivated to accept treatment. Where the disease of alcoholism is concerned, there are several major factors militating against the success of secondary prevention efforts. These are:

(1) The difficulty of early detection. The well-recognised skill of the alcoholic in concealing the problem, combined with the opportunities for protective colouration in a society which not only accepts, but strongly encourages, alcohol as a social lubricant, makes the difficulty of early detection obvious.

(2) Society's continuing tendency to visualise the alcoholic as a 'skid-row' stereotype, to view alcoholism as a 'self-inflicted disease', and to regard the victim as some sort of irresponsible, spineless, morally-weak individual, provides a powerful incentive for the victim to both conceal and deny the existence of the disease.

(3) The powerful nature of the addiction to alcohol (characteristic of this disease) is such that the victim cannot accept the notion that life can be satisfactory without alcohol. The very thought of total abstinence is so terrifying that the motivation for concealment and denial are further reinforced. The validity of this point is strongly supported by the high rate of suicide among alcoholics, demonstrating that even death is often preferable to abstinence.

(4) The deep-seated feelings of guilt, remorse, and shame of the victim, coupled with feelings of hopelessness with respect to abstinence, are powerful preventives to seeking help or accepting treatment.

All the foregoing factors combine to produce a situation which is not usually present in the secondary prevention of disease — the fact that the patient *does not want to be treated.*

The most effective method discovered to date for overcoming these obstacles to identification and ultimate treatment of alcoholism is that utilised in effective employee alcoholism programs. The 'job performance approach' assures early identification of the alcoholic employee. Furthermore, the most effective motivation for getting the alcoholic to do something about the problem remains the alcoholic's desire to keep the job. This motivation is accomplished by offering the employee a firm, fair choice between accepting treatment or accepting the disciplinary consequences of the poor job performance. If any discipline (up to and including dismissal) is administered, it is only at the expressed wish of the employee. The program will not work if the employee *prefers* termination to accepting help.

Fortunately, this seldom occurs. Many alcoholics are likely to be employees with long service and be highly skilled at their jobs. Program results indicate that few will choose termination in the final showdown. Management is thereby saved additional losses which occur when a highly-skilled individual must be dismissed (thus losing a large investment of time and money which was required to bring that individual to that degree of skill) and when more money must be spent to recruit, hire, and train a replacement with absolutely no assurance whatsoever that the replacement does not suffer from the same problem.

Key Program Elements

The list which follows covers specific components which have been found to be essential in maximising program effectiveness. In tailoring any program to meet the needs of a specific organisation the following points should be covered:

(1) The company (and union) have a written policy dealing specifically with *alcoholism alone* — a policy which is known to *all* employees and which clearly delineates a positive procedure aimed at helping alcoholics to recover.

(2) The company has developed specific procedures in regard to the handling and referral of employees experiencing job performance problems, and line management accomplishes compliance with these procedures as a job responsibility of supervisors at all levels.

(3) The program has an effective referral system, i.e. procedures, qualified alcoholism diagnostic facilities, and personnel with the qualifications necessary to assure that alcoholics will be referred to the appropriate rehabilitative agencies.

(4) The program has access to treatment facilities which are appropriate for the employed alcoholic and refers alcoholic employees to these facilities as needed.

(5) The program has set in motion a systematic approach to training supervisors (and union representatives) at all levels, specifically in the procedures they will follow to implement the alcoholism policy, and the exact procedure for making referrals.
(6) The program has an educational component designed to inform employees regarding modern approaches to alcoholism, and one which includes a complete description of the written policy on *alcoholism.*
(7) The program has an effective medical record-keeping system which assures confidentiality to the individual employee, while furnishing evidence of programe effectiveness through reports on numbers of alcoholics identified and successfully motivated to accept treatment. The data used in these reports should permit comparison with results or other operating programs, so as to obtain meaningful measures of program effectiveness. These records should also provide some acceptable measure of the program's cost-effectiveness.
(8) The company (and union) have provided for third-party payment for the treatment of alcoholic employees in their group health insurance policies or other company benefits.

Programs which include all of the above elements are achieving some remarkable results.

As one leading authority has pointed out, treatment is not the problem. Luther A. Cloud, MD, writing in the *Labor-Management Alcoholism Journal*, notes two phenomena in connection with effective 'pre-treatment' programs.

> One dividend of this situation is the fact that, because of the early identification factor, many of the alcoholics who turn up in these programs require virtually no *medical* treatment whatsoever.
> For example, in its first year of operation, the Union Pacific program identified and motivated some 245 alcoholic employees, 78 per cent of whom required *no in-patient treatment of any kind.* Only *five* cases required hospitalization for acute alcoholism (detoxification). (Labour-Management and Alcoholism Journal, 1974b)

Dr Cloud also noted the recovery statistics compiled by one treatment facility which broke down all its employer referrals (from business, industry, and governmental agencies) into two groups, one of which met the eight criteria listed above, and the other of which did not meet all of the criteria or came from employers who did not have any formal programs. The recovery rate reported for the first group was 92 per cent, while that reported for the second group was 52.9 per cent. Both groups went through the identical treatment modality in the identical institution with the identical personnel.

As Dr Cloud observed:

> In any case, long-term, successful recoveries will come, not solely as a result of our 'treatment', but in direct proportion to the effectiveness of the motivation which these programs supply in the 'pre-treatment' phase . . . The key to recovery from alcoholism lies in the hands of enlightened management and union leadership — not in treatment *per se*. (Labour-Management and Alcoholism Journal, 1974b)

Penetration Rates

Today, however, we do not judge a program's effectiveness by its 'recovery rate'. For one thing, ever since the earliest program at du Pont, these employer-based programs have achieved high recovery rates due to the built-in motivational factor. For another, a program which identified only one alcoholic per year and which enabled that individual to achieve recovery would have a 100 per cent recovery rate, but it could hardly be called an *effective* program. Remember that somewhere between five per cent and ten per cent of any work-force has the disease of alcoholism in its early, middle, or late stages.

Therefore, we consider the so-called 'penetration rate' to be the best current measure of true program effectiveness. Penetration rate can be defined as the answer to the following question: What per-centage of your total employee population has been identified as alcoholic *and* motivated to accept treatment in each year of the program's existence?

Using this definition, we believe that, with few exceptions, a properly-designed and implemented, joint, union-management employee alcoholism program which includes the eight key elements listed earlier should achieve a penetration rate ranging between 1.5 per cent and two per cent per year. Many programs in the United States today are achieving a penetration rate of one per cent or more annually.

Some results achieved by modern programs include:

(1) The Boston Post Office in *five* years identified 725 of its total payroll of 9,000 as alcoholics — more than eight per cent. The Los Angeles Post Office identified 2.5 per cent *the first year*!

(2) Kelsey-Hayes in *three* years identified 400 alcoholics in a payroll of 5,000 — an eight per cent figure.

(3) Darrell Sorenson of the Union Pacific Railroad reports that, at the railroad's headquarters in Omaha, Nebraska, 240 of 2,500 employees were taken into the program in the first *four* years — a 9.6 per cent figure.

(4) The City of Lee's Summit, Missouri, at the end of *two* years had counselled 13 alcoholics out of a total employee population of 120 — a figure representing 10.8 per cent of that payroll.

Cost-effectiveness

Another area in which we can measure the effectiveness of employee alcoholism programs is their cost savings. A number of these savings have been reported in the *Labor-Management Alcoholism Journal*. Among them:

(1) The US Postal Service has reported (since the inception of its first program in San Francisco in 1968) an annual return of $5 for every $1 spent on the program — this despite the fact that it is the most extensively-staffed and expensive program in the United States, requiring one counsellor for every 1,500 employees on the payroll. These figures have undergone three federal audits.

(2) Scovill Manufacturing Company reported a *minimum* saving per recovered alcoholic of $3,900 annually, and cited the case of a single alcoholic employee whose absence due to alcoholism cost the company *$27,000 in three days*.

(3) The New York Transit Authority some time ago made a study of 1,600 individuals who had been through their program. Only one item was considered — paid sick leave. On that item alone, the Authority was then saving over $1 million per year in that group.

(4) Early returns from the General Motors program showed

reductions of 85.5 per cent in lost man-hours; 72.0 per cent in the dollar amount of accident and sickness disability benefits paid, and 46.7 per cent in number of sick leaves taken.

(5) The Oldsmobile program, cited earlier, found a *reduction of 82 per cent in on-the-job accidents* among the alcoholics who had been counselled.

(6) A large, international corporation which is not yet ready to publish its results, reports estimated savings of $20 for every $1 spent on implementation of the program. This company did a special study on a small group of alcoholics at the managerial or executive level in their corporate headquarters, who would have been dismissed had it not been for their participation in the program. Only those individuals were included who had achieved successful recoveries. Only one item was considered — the amount which would have had to be given to these individuals in severance pay if they had been terminated (as would have been the case had there been no program). It was discovered that *on this one item alone* the company saved enough money to pay for *all* of its employee alcoholism programs throughout the world.

In view of the fact that results like these are possible, it would seem that all employers would be eager to start alcoholism programs for their employees. Yet even after 37 years, this has not happened. In fact, out of approximately 1,800,000 corporations in the United States, probably not more than 3,000 have such programs today. The myths and stigma surrounding the disease of alcoholism persist. Employers still say things like: 'We don't have that problem in our organisation!' or, 'If we find an alcoholic, we fire that individual.'

The first statement ignores the fact that 95 per cent of alcoholic employees are not 'visible' as such. The second ignores a principle which has been amply documented: if you find an alcoholic on your payroll, the most expensive thing you can do at that point is to fire that individual.

We have a tremendous job ahead of us which involves educating management to the fact that it *cannot afford not to have* alcoholism programs. Our situation is analogous to that of the experts who were advocating 'safety programs' a few years ago. Today, an employer without a safety program is considered to be behind the times. Perhaps tomorrow, an employer without an employee alcoholism program will be looked on in the same light.

10 INDUSTRIAL ALCOHOL PROGRAMS IN NORWAY

Fanny Duckert

In 1977 the Norwegian population over 15 years of age on average consumed about 5.7 litres of spirits (Statens Edruskapsdirektorat, 1978) and spent 5.1 million crowns on alcoholic beverages, this latter figure being nearly twice as much as in 1972 even allowing for inflation. Further, it is generally considered that over ten per cent of the Norwegian population over 15 years of age have problems related to alcohol and, as the majority of these are people in their prime in relation to the capability for work, this means that alcohol-related problems at work must occur in Norwegian industry. It is uncertain as to whether alcoholism and alcohol abuse are more widespread now than before, but what is clear however is that alcohol-related problems are likely to be more serious today in industry because of increased technological development with advanced machinery, complicated automation and synchronised, highly-specialised work. In this situation the effort of an individual operator can often be decisive to a whole production and working levels often require exactitude and reliability of a much higher degree than before.

Effects of Alcohol in Norwegian Industry

It is speculated that 340 million Norwegian crowns (approximately £30 million) each year are lost because of absenteeism due to excessive alcohol consumption (Borg, 1970). Unfortunately in relation to industrial accidents it is not possible due to absence of statistics to measure the degree to which alcohol and other drugs are a cause of accidents. However, the link between traffic accidents and alcohol is clear (Andenaes and Sørensen, 1979) and it is believed that alcohol-related industrial accidents do occur. This is supported by the frequency of accidents at work occurring more frequently on Mondays and after holidays, i.e. periods of heavy drinking. Whilst alcohol consumption may not be as high in Norway as in other countries there is concern in industry both in relation to absenteeism and to accidents. Further, Norway has a history of taking alcohol problems seriously and over

161

the years different industrial alcohol programs have been developed, some of which are reviewed here.

The AKAN Program

AKAN (the Committee of Industry and Trade) against alcoholism and drug addiction was established in 1963 on the joint initiative of the employers confederation and the trade unions in an effort to handle problems in industry and trade caused by the excessive use of alcohol and drugs.

The aims of AKAN are first, to prevent alcoholism and drug addiction and secondly, to help alcoholics and drug addicts return to a normal life. The Committee has five members of which two are appointed by the Employers Confederation, two by trade unions and one by the state through the Ministry of Social Affairs. In the bye-laws of the organisation it is laid down that a representative of one of the two organisations alternatively shall serve as chairman. The state pays one half of the committee's expenses whilst the other half is met by the two organisations. The aim of AKAN is thus to take part in the prevention of alcoholism and drug addiction through information and education and to help those with problems to return to a normal life as soon as possible.

This work is done independently and does not attempt to replace the work done by other organisations nor does it aim to promote special viewpoints of teetotal organisations. On the contrary AKAN tries to arrange for sober and factual information to be provided to industry and trade. AKAN uses educational means such as pamphlets and arranges courses and conferences for interested persons in industry and trade during which the participants are informed of the development of alcoholism and drug addiction and also of the many problems arising for those who abuse these substances. Further, AKAN will give advice and guidance to individual enterprises and/or works committees in connection with actual management of clients with alcohol problems.

It is generally known throughout the country that use or abuse of intoxicating substances at the place of work in Norway is forbidden and if discovered may lead to instantaneous dismissal. AKAN's intention is that in relation to such work regulations, an exception can be made if an alcohol or drug abuser voluntarily accepts help and treatment offered. A range of help may be offered including

individual counselling, medical treatment, family support, inpatient
or outpatient treatment and aftercare. Such help becomes part of the
policy of the industrial enterprise and applies to all employees.
Differences in treatment of abusers is avoided and such people can also
be detected earlier.

As a result of the work undertaken by AKAN more than 30,000
people have been given information about alcohol and narcotic problems
and it is hoped that this has resulted in their greater understanding of
those afflicted with these disorders. It is hoped and indeed believed
that this has resulted in a change to a more positive attitude and also
has encouraged individual employees with these problems to seek
help. At present more than 500 industrial enterprises, including
both state and private, employing more than 100,000 people have
established AKAN programs. In effect therefore the AKAN program
resembles programs in other countries in that it not only provides a combination of education about alcoholism and drug addiction for industrial
employees but also offers rehabilitation programs. It has to be
admitted that as the carrying out of the AKAN program is generally
done by the staff of the individual industrial enterprise, the quality
of the program, depending as it does on the knowledge and skill of
such staff, is often variable. It is indeed questionable in some of the
AKAN projects whether there is sufficient professional guidance and
supervision of employees.

The AKAN program, as with other programs such as those in the
United States, is primarily concerned to detect and help those who
have alcohol and drug problems as well as to provide general
education. Frequently the problem exists however as to what to do
with people who have already got into serious difficulties and indeed
have lost jobs through alcohol and drug problems and in Norway this
problem has been dealt with in a very sensible way.

Work Training Groups

The ISO Groups

These groups which began in Oslo in 1974 were formed on the initiative
of a group of therapists and social workers who were involved in the
treatment and rehabilitation of young alcoholics and drug addicts in
the Oslo area. They felt that their own work with such young people
was of little avail unless there was a possibility of employment and
they carried out negotiations with the Directorate of Labour about
establishing work training groups for such young people who had

difficulty in obtaining work.

The ISO groups were originally based on a Danish model from Aarhus (Arbeidsdirektoratet, 7, 1979). They offer work to young people under the age of 25 who have difficulties in getting and keeping jobs because of their abuse of drugs or alcohol and/or other social or psychological problems. The trainees may be recruited from treatment institutions, social services offices and labour offices and the total period of training initially lasts three months. The young people work in groups of eight trainees under a work leader who is usually a social worker with a good knowledge of the labour market. Such a social worker plays a very important role as an adult model figure to be imitated. The jobs are provided by the Council of Oslo and consist of mainly outdoor activities such as the cleaning up of parks and forest areas, restoration of old buildings, painting, gardening, etc. The participants get ordinary wages paid partly by the Directorate of Labour and partly by the local administration. The management of the training groups is done by a project manager in co-operation with a multi-disciplinary team consisting of group leaders, physician, social worker and rehabilitation officer.

The purpose of the ISO group is to train youngsters with little previous work experience to work with basic skills, so that they learn to change their life-style from unstructured idleness to structured occupation. They are taught to remain at work throughout the whole day, to handle tools, obey orders and carry out work which will be supervised, to learn to co-operate with others and give adequate reasons for absenteeism etc.

The groups are closed groups with the same participants carrying out the work throughout the same period. This helps of course with identification and solidarity, and this is regarded as an important part of the training process. These youngsters are often recruited from a very tough environment where everyone is used to looking after themselves and where trust and responsibility for others is rarely taken or given. The aim of the group training is to change this and make trainees think of themselves as ordinary people with ordinary responsibilities and confidence in others. In the group interpersonal problems and conflicts are handled as part of their training. There is close co-operation with social workers outside the training groups, so that when the young people leave the group they may be followed up in their natural environment.

The ISO groups provide an extensive work training program providing an integral alternative to institutionalisation for such young people.

Following the training period the trainees are helped to obtain ordinary jobs or further training by the rehabilitation officer using group methods but of a less directive kind.

Up to 1978, 22 work training groups have been carried out in Oslo comprising of about 250 youngsters. Of these two-thirds had addictions as their main problem and about 60 per cent became engaged in work or continued satisfactorily in a further educational program after their initial training. The ISO groups are widely accepted as successful and in addition to the groups in Oslo similar groups have been started in about seven other cities in Norway. There are problems however with the program concerning the closed nature of the group. Thus when people leave, the numbers in the group become very low and unsatisfactory therapeutically. Further, the difficulties that face the group leader in taking such individual young people from a range of different backgrounds and in fact bringing them together in a cohesive group are immense, particularly during a period as short as three months.

The Valo Project

Originally the Valo project (Lanesskog, 1978) was a private humanitarian organisation called Operasjon Ved (Operation Wood). The purpose of this was to distribute free wood to elderly and handicapped people in the Oslo area, the work being done by volunteers. It was suggested in 1975 that such work could be carried out by unemployed young people and today the project is exclusively a work training therapeutic project for persons with problems, especially young people and particularly those with alcohol and drug problems. The Council of Oslo pays the cost of the enterprise whilst the employment office takes care of the practical administration of the project. Operasjon Ved, the original private organisation, now has a minimal influence on the project.

Today altogether 74 people are employed on the project and the trainees again work in groups with a work leader. They cut trees, carry out forestry work and work for the local administration doing gardening, cleaning, painting and carpeting. At the beginning new trainees are given simple tasks like wood-chopping, but later they may be promoted to more advanced and responsible tasks. To become a member of the project the person must have a history of problems at work, must be over 16 years of age and must have someone in a community willing to monitor him. Selection interviews of prospective clients take place, but it is rare that applicants are turned down. Once appointed the person obtains a contract for six months which can be repeated once. If promoted to a specialised trainee post then he may get a further contract of six months that can also be renewed once more. If an employee is fired for violating working rules, he may re-apply for work after a period of six weeks. The aim is to make the work tasks as similar to that of ordinary industry as possible and the trainees are thus treated as employees having similar rules for absenteeism, holidays, sickness leave, etc.

During 1978, 173 clients (140 men and 33 women) participated in the project — their mean age being 28 years and mean time in the project being 100 days for women and 79 days for men. About one-third of the clients were self-referral cases, the remainder having been referred from parts of the social services and labour departments. One hundred of the clients had alcohol and drug problems. A survey carried out in 1977 of this sort of group showed that they came from a very deprived educational background, had low vocational status, long periods of unemployment and low levels of social functioning together with serious problems of alcohol and drug abuse.

It is important to realise that this project represents a rare offer to alcohol and drug addicts, a group usually rejected by employers as suitable for either training or employment in general. An encouraging result of the project has been how these young people have responded and worked well. Follow-up studies carried out three months after training have shown that during 1978 45 per cent were in stable work. In relation to their general social functioning including levels of education it was felt that 53 per cent had made satisfactory social improvement. The Valo project however also has problems, e.g. placing so many people with addictive problems together produces the problem of alcohol and drug use during working hours and also may encourage progression from minor drug use to major drug use through direct contact. Again administrators and therapists on the project find the work very demanding. The project is usually administered by a psychologist.

The ALKO Project

From March 1975 to December 1977 a joint project was carried out with the Directorate of Labour in relation to the rehabilitation department of the Employment Office in Oslo. The purpose of this experiment (the ALKO project) was to try out different methods of rehabilitation of alcohol and drug addicts. A multi-disciplinary team involving physicians, psychologists, rehabilitation officers, social

workers, insurance officer and a research assistant who was a past
alcohol-abuser was set up, the team being responsible for the development and carrying through of the project. Contact and cross-
fertilisation were obtained from institutions such as hospitals, social
welfare officers, prisons and industry. The basic aim was to recruit
clients from the Temperance Welfare, i.e. lower-class alcoholics and
drug addicts of whom many could be categorised as being on skid-row.
Generally this group has been looked on as having a very poor prognosis
and has received very little assistance from treatment and rehabilitation
facilities.

The aim was to carry out help on an outpatient basis for at least
six months, the basic theoretical framework being social learning
theory, addiction being considered not as a disease but as a learned
disorder and part of a certain lifestyle. The changing of drinking
pattern or drug abusing habits was therefore only one of the goals that
the client has to achieve. Little interest was taken in the background
of the client, the focus being on the 'here and now', and the individual
rehabilitation program being based on an improvement on the 'here
and now' situation. The particular type of abuse was considered to be
of very little importance and therefore alcoholics and drug addicts
could join the same program. One hundred and seventeen individuals
(90 men and 27 women), aged 17 to 55 were selected. This selection
however was done randomly. Fifty-four per cent were mainly alcohol
abusers, 20 per cent drug abusers and 26 per cent used both alcohol
and drugs. The group was characterised by a long-standing history of
addiction, previous hospitalisations, a fairly high degree of registered
criminal activity (e.g. more than half the group had been in prison),
incomplete or marginal education and long periods of unemployment.
Indeed the majority had been out of work for more than six months
when referred.

In relation to the alcohol abusers skid-row alcoholics were the
predominant group. The design of each rehabilitation program was
based upon a thorough analysis of the client's present situation and
needs. The major components in the plan were employment, education and therapeutic techniques based on behaviour therapy. The
most important employment strategies were regular employment,
often with subsidised wages or sheltered employment in ordinary
enterprises or work training in special small groups as with the ISO
and VALO projects or work carried out in sheltered enterprises for
the disabled. In addition to work it was felt that education was very
important since many clients had a very impoverished educational

background. Often it was necessary to start with special tuition individually or in small groups to bring clients to a level where they
could attend levels of ordinary education. In addition there were
courses for six months organised by the Labour Office aimed at giving
practical competence on the regular labour market. As often as
possible ordinary courses and schools of all levels were used. In essence
therefore by direct training in relation to work and education but with
little attempt at insight, the aim was to rehabilitate people and by
changing their overall lifestyle they would be expected to lose their
past lifestyle including taking alcohol and drugs.

Earlier on it was of interest that the majority of clients neither
cared for nor profited from more traditional insight therapy. This has
also been supported by other studies (Orford and Edwards, 1977).
In the beginning these people had often been referred for psychiatric
treatment but had had very disappointing experiences. Instead it was
felt that the natural surroundings of the new environment were used
therapeutically. By using these they learned to solve acute problems
and crises facing them at work, at home and in contact with other
people without having to go into hospitals or institutions. The
strategy was to go through the different types of situation that
people were likely to find themselves in by making a careful analysis
of the problems involved and their own individual ability. Often
contracts were made outlining specific aims and how to reach them,
dividing tasks, responsibilities and rights between the clients and
other persons involved including employer, family members, social
workers, etc. Plans were also made to anticipate problems and events,
e.g. a drinking relapse. The point here was to make drinking less
pleasant and sobriety more so without rejecting a person when
drunk. There was also extensive use made of social training procedures
such as role play and home lessons to build up clients' social repertoires

At regular intervals feedback meetings were held with the client
and other people involved, discussing problems and positive developments, adjusting contracts or making new ones. The eventual goal was
to make the clients gradually more able to take responsibility for
their own lives by learning how to handle their everyday problems.
It was important not to give the clients tasks that were beyond them
and to do everything in a careful manner and as far as possible
attention was paid to their own wishes and requests. There was complete openness in everything concerning their own case in letting
them read documents and participate in meetings, and in informing
them of their rights etc. Too often clients in the past had met staff

who made decisions for them, and made unrealistic demands and rejected them if they failed. Slowly the self-confidence and ability to solve problems of these people was built up, the aim being to develop alternative social strategies and an increased feeling of confidence in handling their lives. Extensive use was made of local resources like social officers, employers and health insurance officers.

Results

For every client the last twelve months prior to entrance in the rehabilitation program was compared with the time spent in the program using the following measures:

(1) time spent in vocational activity, work education;
(2) use of alcohol and drugs;
(3) registered criminal activity;
(4) housing situation; and
(5) time spent in inpatient institutions.

The data were collected through the client's self-reports and also from public sources such as police, health insurance officers, social welfare employers, social workers, friends and family.

Of the total group three died during the project time and 17 clients had incomplete data and had to be excluded, so that 97 persons remained in the group. Because clients ended the program at different points in time, the time spent in the program varied from six to 24 months, but none had spent less than six months and they stopped receiving new clients six months before the end of the program.

The results shown in Figure 10.1 indicate that the clients in their year before referral were in a situation characterised by criminal activity, homelessness, long periods of time in institutions, low vocational activity and heavy use of alcohol and drugs. After entrance into the rehabilitation program however, clients showed a marked tendency towards increased vocational activity and less alcohol and drug abuse. Also less time was spent in inpatient institutions and registered criminal activity decreased. In relation to recorded criminal activity, the mean number of arrests and charges was 1.26 the year before referral to the project. During the first year of the project this mean fell to 0.54 and during the second year to 0.24.

This positive development was somewhat surprising as the social

Figure 10.1: Changes in Clients' Social Functioning During the Period of the Project Compared with the Previous Year

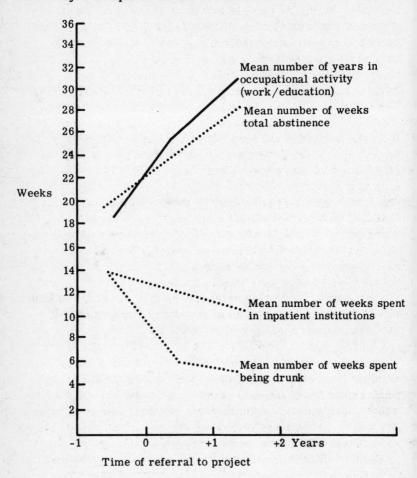

Note

In relation to recorded criminal activity, mean number of arrests and charges was 1.26 the year before referral to the project. During the first year of the project this mean fell to 0.54 and during the second year to 0.24.

environment, including housing for the majority of the group, was still unsatisfactory at the end of the project, principally due to the general housing shortage in the Oslo area which makes it very difficult to acquire a flat. Clients showed an ability to change their lifestyle even under poor living conditions such as boarding houses and hostels situated in slum areas. Only to a small extent did they have the protection against alcohol, drugs or criminality that is normally provided by living in an institution. Interestingly enough these changes also seem to be quite stable for some of the clients, at least for two years. The ALKO project is a pilot project designed to last three years in all and the methods used are not necessarily easily incorporated into regular rehabilitation services. The principal aim of it was to show that even skid-row-type clients have an ability to improve their level of functioning if they can get the right kind of help. Lessons learnt from the ALKO project have been distributed to all labour offices and social services offices in Norway and it is felt that a great deal has been learnt about how to work with the rehabilitation of drug addicts and alcoholics. Several of the measures carried out by the ALKO project have now been worked into the regular work rehabilitation services, the most important of these being the following.

First, there is the establishing of multi-professional teams to handle rehabilitation cases in the labour offices, thus securing a more rapid and comprehensive handling of these cases.

Secondly, there is extensive use of sheltered employment in ordinary enterprises as an alternative to separate sheltered workshops. These are especially suitable for the rehabilitation of addicts for whom the traditional sheltered workshops are not a good alternative. When wages are subsidised, the employer usually is more prepared to give the client a break and this also allows for more flexible working arrangements giving where necessary training possibilities.

Thirdly, it has become easier to finance rehabilitation programs for addicts from insurance offices. The Directorate of Labour has granted money for subsidies and loans to rehabilitation programs for clients in difficult situations. These monies are administered by multi-professional teams. It seems a more optimistic view upon addicts on what can be done once rehabilitation has started. Today addicts are widely accepted as regular rehabilitation clients with problems connected with work and usually receive the same service as other clients.

Summary

In Norway there developed different rehabilitation programs aimed at the rehabilitation of alcoholics in industry. The most important of these is the AKAN program, this program being specifically aimed at alcohol abusers still in employment. For alcohol abusers no longer in work the Directorate of Labour has established different programs of which the ISO group, Valo group and the ALKO project have been the most important, helping to rehabilitate the unemployed alcohol addict.

11 FRENCH APPROACHES TO ALCOHOL PROBLEMS IN EMPLOYMENT

Jacques Godard

Alcohol problems are currently regarded as a response to biological, psychological and social factors. Such problems are of major concern because of their frequency and their gravity and a wide range of disabilities is involved. Alcohol problems occur virtually everywhere and under all conditions. In consequence these problems should be prevented or ameliorated on an equally grand scale, including in the work setting.

This assertion may be debated on ideological grounds, particularly in the name of individual freedom, or of medical etiquette, or in the name of industrial expediency. Even so, there seems to be a broad popular consensus in France and in many other industrialised countries that positive approaches to alcohol problems in employment should be carefully established and gradually implemented.

Justifications

Two questions require to be answered at the beginning of this review. The first is directed at the employer. The second one is directed to trade unions.

1. Should Management (in Whatever Type of Employment, Manufacturing, Commerce, Private or Publicly-owned) Do Anything to Curb Alcohol Problems?

Without doubt the answer is 'yes'. As J.L. Norris, formerly Chief Physician at Eastman Kodak (Rochester, New York) once said: 'The directors of a corporation who claim that there are no alcohol problems among their staff do not know what they are talking about.' (Norris, 1972). There are, in fact, excessive drinkers in all occupations. It has recently been estimated that 12 to 15 per cent of the male working population and at least five per cent of working females in France are excessive drinkers. Research may produce comparable results elsewhere and, as noted in Chapter 2, certain occupations have particularly high rates of alcohol problems. Such problems are not always conspicuous. Sometimes they are not visible due to reluctance to identify them. All too often problem drinkers in employment are ignored or tolerated, until finally they are punished or dismissed if they become an embarrassment. This solution is wasteful and inhumane, although as a short-term expedient the approach may sometimes be attractive to management. Socially, nothing is resolved for the town, region or country. Society is then forced to support the invalid and industry will contribute, indirectly, to the collective cost of this burden. If a sick, discarded worker becomes seriously ill the cost to society increases.

Alcohol problems can be overcome, especially if they are identified and handled in a constructive and realistic way at the earliest possible stage. Early intervention is also likely to be the cheapest type to implement. As noted in Chapter 1, excessive drinking is a major cause of absenteeism, ill health, accidents, loss of efficiency and possibly of poor industrial relations. Another reason for managements to adopt constructive approaches to alcohol problems in employment is that since 11 October 1946, it has been law in France that the worker's health should be monitored to ensure that he is fit to cope with his job and not a danger either to himself or to others.

2. Should Trade Unions Attempt to Curb Alcohol Problems?

The answer to this question must also be 'yes'.

The harmful, even tragic, consequences of excessive drinking sometimes afflict the less-privileged members of society most harshly. Sometimes harsh work conditions, either physical or mental, contribute to the development of alcohol problems. If workers are harmed in this way their capacity to defend their rights and standard of living will be eroded. In addition, problem drinkers may often justifiably be regarded as victims of a situation not of their own making. They thereby deserve the assistance and sympathy of their colleagues. It is part of the responsibility of trade unions to supply workers with information to protect their general well-being and this includes information about this major industrial problem.

Alcohol problems are a topic upon which management and trade unions should be able to co-operate and acknowledge a common interest. Both sides of industry should consequently devise a mutually-beneficial program of action. Evidence is now available that indicates which approaches may be adopted most fruitfully.

Choice of Methods

It is evident that alcohol problems must be managed as a collaborative venture.

1. Who Should be Involved?

(1) The management of the company and the senior company officials — without such co-operation little could be achieved.

(2) Technical staff and section managers nearer to the workers. These may be more in touch with what happens at a 'grass roots' level.

(3) Shop stewards and foremen whose participation is indispensible. Very often in Western countries such individuals have more moral influence in the workplace than do senior managers or directors.

(4) Those responsible for specialised services in the workplace. These include company doctors and nurses (if any), security guards and personnel staff.

(5) Finally, fellow workers, Often the workforce includes members of self-help groups such as Alcoholics Anonymous (AA), former problem drinkers, or others who can provide help. This is often available even if the company does not have its own formal AA group.

2. How Is a Successful Approach Achieved?

It is apparent that leaflets, posters and films used without preparation have little effect unless three conditions are fulfilled:

(1) A responsible initiator and co-ordinator of action to deal with alcohol problems has to be chosen. This may be the managing director if that individual is sufficiently interested in being committed to the implementation of a company policy on alcohol problems. The identity of the co-ordinator will vary from company to company. Sometimes it may be the company doctor, nurse, personnel manager, a foreman, etc. The co-ordinator may be appointed to this task either on a full- or part-time basis, depending on the size of the firm. Sometimes this work will be aided by one or several associates.

(2) Initially those individuals who appear most amenable to the establishment of a program to overcome alcohol problems at work will have to be identified. Their co-operation and assistance will have to be enlisted in adopting a practical common course of

action.

(3) Considerable time must, if necessary, be invested in winning the support of influential people within the company, in particular trade union officials or other workers' representatives. In this respect a 'personal approach' is indispensible and is certainly the best way of achieving a sympathetic and friendly understanding of the proposed approach. Considerable diplomacy and initiative are required in convincing people of the common advantages of such an approach. Very often younger people respond more enthusiastically, regardless of whether they are white-collar or blue-collar workers or trade union officials. Generally such individuals provide most of the support for industry-based schemes to deal with alcohol problems.

3. How is a Program Planned?

(1) A responsible organisation must be selected. This will vary in different settings. In France the Workers' Welfare Association often performs this role, either at central or local branch levels.

(2) A program of action will be outlined for a limited period such as one year. Policy will be periodically reviewed and, if necessary, revised if this is required after critical appraisal.

(3) One possibility is to organise annually a week or even a single day of sobriety. In France companies have done this in co-operation with the Hygiene and Security Committee.

(4) Finally, as much help as possible should be sought from organisations or resources outside the company, including National Health Service prevention and treatment facilities, local councils on alcoholism, AA groups and any organisations providing help or advice for problem drinkers. All such bodies can usefully be consulted to formulate the precise objectives and methods to be used in general, and for each person in need of help.

Prevention

Preventive strategies should pursue five major directions:

1. Information about the Effects and Potential Dangers of Alcohol

In essence this should aim to refute the most widespread misconceptions about drinking and alcohol problems.

Specifically it should be explained that alcohol problems are not confined to drunkenness, but also include prolonged and excessive (or inappropriate) drinking. Very often an individual will not exhibit striking symptoms and may only gradually and over a considerable period of time suffer physical or psychological damage. 'Stronger' or more concentrated drinks such as spirits, liqueurs, etc. are by no means the only alcoholic beverages that can be misused or lead to harmful consequences. In France it is pointed out that four litres of normal wine are equivalent at least to a litre of brandy. In Britain one could explain that there is as much alcohol in a normal pint of beer as there is in a double whisky. Alcohol does not provide strength since it does not sustain the muscles. The anaesthetic effects of alcohol often mislead drinkers into assuming that it aids vigilance. In fact, as noted in Chapter 1, alcohol is a depressant and slows reactions down. If the drinker is unaware of these effects accidents may result. Alcohol is not thirst-quenching. On the contrary it produces dehydration and increases the need for water. As the old proverb aptly says: 'The more one drinks, the thirstier one becomes.'

Alcohol does not warm one up, except in a very superficial sense. By dilating the outer blood vessels alcohol creates a glow which only results in reducing body temperature. In some circumstances such as accidents, such heat loss can be highly dangerous unless compensated for. It can be fatal to give alcohol to a person injured, for example, in a mountaineering accident. Sugar is better than rum.

Alcohol is not a medicine. There is no scientific justification for its use as such. Except in the case of severe physical withdrawal symptoms (such as delirium tremens) there is no evidence that people become ill due to alcohol deprivation. Conversely, there are huge numbers of people who have become ill due to excessive drinking.

2. To Teach the Three Main Rules of Sobriety

Drinking alcohol should be optional, moderate and circumstantial.

Optional. Man's natural drink is water. Many people are content with this beverage, or with the huge range of non-alcoholic drinks. One should never put pressure on a person to consume alcoholic drinks. One never knows who another person may be; primarily an abstinent alcoholic or who, for some other reason, is unable to drink without risk (such as a nervous invalid, an epileptic, or somebody with a stomach ulcer). As noted in Chapter 2 some jobs, such as the drink trade, being a commercial traveller or a waiter, subject people to unusual pressure to drink. Moderation is a necessity for such people for whom excessive drinking may be a major occupational hazard. On all occasions one should make available soft as well as alcoholic drinks. Above all, never force somebody to consume alcohol.

Moderate. The daily maximum reasonable dose for healthy adult males is between 0.5 and 0.75 litres of 10° wine. The corresponding dose for females is between 0.25 and 0.5 litres of the equivalent in the form of other drinks. Such (optional) consumption should ideally accompany meals and ideally one should avoid 'appetisers' or 'digestives'. Alcohol should be avoided between meals and at all times if one has to drive. Alcohol should be avoided by pregnant women or by mothers who are breast feeding as well as by young people under the legal age at which alcohol consumption is permitted.

Circumstantial. One may set general limits for alcohol consumption. These may, *occasionally*, be broken. Such events may be acceptable provided they are only very rare and provided one does not cause risk to oneself or to others, for example, by driving while under the influence of alcohol or entering some other potentially risky situation.

3. Improvement of Working Conditions

Fatigue, monotony and boredom at work certainly contribute to excessive drinking in the work setting. Every improvement of working conditions may serve to reduce the pressures to misuse alcohol. Industrial strategies to prevent alcohol problems should take into account the physical and mental demands, lighting, routines, comfort and safety, noise, temperature and pollution. Sometimes a hot or dusty working environment will stimulate a need for thirst-quenching refreshment. Traditionally this need has often been met by alcoholic drinks, which in fact are counterproductive as explained above. For such reasons it is valuable to gain the co-operation of those concerned with regulating the conditions of work.

4. Sensible Diet

It should be ensured that workers obtain a satisfactory and adequate diet both in quantity and quality. In particular, adequate provision should be made of non-alcoholic liquid. Sometimes the following strategies are warranted:

(1) To provide staff canteens or restaurants with properly-designed balanced menus of well-cooked dishes. Alcohol consumption should be limited and sensible guidelines suggested and

publicised for 'acceptable' or 'sensible' drinking.

(2) To provide dining rooms near locker rooms and rest rooms for individuals who bring their own food to work. Ideally such rooms should be equipped with a refrigerator, a cooker and drinkable water.

(3) To install a snack bar or vending machines for sandwiches, biscuits, etc.

5. Drinks

The consumption of alcohol at work is sufficiently strictly-regulated even if such regulations are frequently not properly-enforced. Even so, progress is being made in this field in particular by the combined efforts of the Factories Inspectorate (a department of the Department of Employment) and the National Committee for Protection against Alcoholism, aided by numerous managements and groups of workers. Current legislation prohibits the supply of alcoholic drinks at work except wine, beer and cider which do not contain added alcohol. In addition, legislation limits the amount of alcohol that a worker is permitted to bring to work. Usually this is either half a litre of wine or a litre of beer during eight working hours. Additional regulations specify that alcohol may be banned from the work environment as a security precaution. Furthermore, since 1960 it has been illegal for companies to give alcoholic drinks as 'fringe benefits' in the workplace.

Workers should always have available accessible fresh water or at least non-alcoholic drinks either at cost price or free of charge. It is a legal requirement that such cheap or free non-alcoholic drinks should be provided whenever working conditions are dry, hot or dusty, or exposed to bad weather. In addition the provision of alcoholic drinks in vending machines is illegal. These legal regulations must be posted up in places of work and the names of those responsible in each company for the enforcement of these rules should also be displayed.

This selective summary outlines the main points that have accompanied the development of the current French approach to alcohol problems in employment. Recently the overall level of alcohol consumption in France has *declined* slightly. It appears now that most consumption is in cafes or at home, whereas at the beginning of the twentieth century most alcohol was consumed at work.

Medical and Social Action

This consists of identifying excessive drinkers and striving to enable them to overcome their problems or preventing further relapses.

The Company Doctor

In the French industrial context the role of the company doctor is primordial.

During annual health inspections or on other occasions, he attempts to identify excessive drinkers at the earliest possible stage. This can be facilitated by recourse to a physical health examination that is widely used in France (as noted below). This examination has the merit that it traces the development of physical ill health due to excessive drinking. In addition it involves the individual worker by presenting him with information about his condition. This may be valuable since the harmful effects of excessive drinking are not always conspicuous and may remain dormant for protracted periods. The clinical examination is completed with liver function tests applied to blood samples. Those tests most commonly used are *mean red cell volume* (MCV) and *gamma glutamyl transpeptidase* (γ-GT). It is obviously of great value to have the evidence of such biological tests since these provide valuable information long before serious or permanent physical damage is caused by excessive drinking. A complete medical profile may be produced by the additional application of psychological tests and a general psychological assessment. It may be important to examine what degree, if any, of mental impairment has been caused. Such considerations are important in deciding what types of work an individual is capable of carrying out competently and safely.

The company doctor may ask the personnel department to elicit discreetly information about a worker's home life or any relevant factors outside work that might cause susceptibility to alcohol problems. Sometimes the assistance of technical staff and supervisors may be obtained, not as a disciplinary step, but to provide further help or support for a worker with alcohol problems. The company doctor also has a role in prevention. This involves disseminating information about the warning signs of alcohol problems or excessive drinking (as noted in Chapter 1). This dissemination should be directed not only at technical staff and section heads, but to all responsible workers and if possible to the entire workforce.

The Medico-social Team

Whatever the composition of the team in the company (doctor, nurse, psychologist, social worker, voluntary counsellor and, in particular, former problem drinkers who are now abstinent) the objective must be:

(1) To track down excessive drinkers and to send them to the nearest and most suitable source of help. Very often such help will have to be provided from outside the company.

(2) Detoxification or 'drying out' is only part of the solution. Frequently this will only be a first step. The main hurdle to overcome is that of motivating the excessive drinker to moderate his alcohol consumption.

(3) It is often asserted that the 'cure' is not as important as what follows, once the excessive drinker is impressed by the dangers of his previous drinking pattern and strives to change. It is sometimes helpful if the excessive drinker can be allocated to work that is not unduly physically or mentally stressful. Such a step may reduce the pressures that could foster a relapse. It is vital that whatever job the (former) excessive drinker should perform, his colleagues should be aware of his problem and never encourage him to drink. Clearly it will be most supportive if they themselves are either moderate drinkers or abstainers.

(4) It must also be ensured that, while on the road to recovery and thereafter, the (former) excessive drinker should adopt a sensible diet. Very often excessive drinkers have neglected their diet for many years. Company medical staff or those from some outside agency should monitor physical health during the recovery period. Sometimes it is supportive and helpful to join AA.

A New Frame of Mind

Before an impact can be made on industrial alcohol problems it is necessary to establish a new climate of opinion towards alcohol and what constitutes unacceptable drinking. Even if a better climate of opinion can be created some people will continue to be vulnerable to drinking excessively.

There is evidence of real progress from many French companies. Such advances are not due to the efforts of a select few. They are certainly attributable to collective activity. The following are the main hallmarks of such activity.

(1) Alcohol problems, a major social malaise, need to be actively combatted by everyone. This requires a radical departure from the collusion and cover-up that is so widespread in relation to excessive drinking.

(2) Problem drinkers should be regarded sympathetically as deserving help and not punitively as degenerate and malicious individuals.

(3) Problem drinkers need to be assisted to surmount their difficulties, to take proper care of themselves, to develop a sense of humour, yet to recognise and compensate for their limitations.

(4) Foremen and shop stewards should be convinced that to identify excessive drinkers for those providing help to such individuals is not an act of betrayal but an act of goodwill.

(5) It must be acknowledged that relapses often occur. These need not be regarded as disasters and should be accepted as a cause for concern and a reason for help, not censure.

(6) Industrial disciplinary procedures should only be resorted to as a last resort. Before recourse to such expedients all 'informal' solutions should be tried.

(7) Drinking problems do not give people immunity from vitally-important industrial safety requirements. These must, at all costs, be maintained.

(8) Finally, sobriety, meaning optional, moderate and circumstantial drinking, should be established as the accepted norm of behaviour by all workers at whatever level and in all types of employment setting.

The New Healthy Diet Centres

Drs Le Go and Pertusier (1971), on behalf of the French Railways, have devised a diet and health examination designed to identify excessive drinkers amongst railway workers. This test is now widely used, especially in industry (see Table 11.1).

This approach, in spite of its merits, gained general acceptance only very gradually. Only during the past five years due to pressure from the National Committee for Defence against Alcoholism have 100 centres been established to carry out such examinations to detect excessive drinkers in employment. The scope and purpose of these examinations are specified in a Ministerial Circular of 31 July 1975. The centres (literally called 'Healthy Diet Centres') are primarily intended to be receptive preventive agencies. They must fulfil three

Table 11.1: The Le Go Test

	Appearance			Tremulousness		
	F Face	P Pupils	T Tongue	M Mouth	T Tongue	E Extremities
Main Signs						
	Subjective Disorders			Liver	Weight Height	Blood pressure
	Nervous	Digestive	Motor coordination			
Additional Signs						

requirements:

(1) Provide a medical and social staff highly-motivated and fully-trained to cope with alcohol problems.

(2) Organise continuous and vigorous recruitment of excessive drinkers from industry. This aim is assisted by doctors and others in industry, in hospitals and in the community.

(3) Ensure that the costs of the service are provided by arrangement with the regional services providing facilities for problem drinkers. These depend upon both statutory grants and financial support from private agencies such as industrial companies.

It is essential that such a service is highly co-ordinated with psychiatric agencies, Alcoholics Anonymous, other non-statutory bodies and general practitioners who often refer people to the centres. It is considered important that the centres should attract people at the earliest stages of their excessive drinking. They are not primarily intended for those in the final stages of alcohol-induced ill health.

The centres should have at their disposal an adequate staff comprised of various professionals (doctors, nurses, social workers, etc.) to be able to provide a 24-hour, seven-day-a-week service. In addition they should have resources to permit staff to visit clients in their own homes and to follow them up as long as required. Doctors and other staff attached to such centres should be provided with ongoing training to ensure that they acquire the optimum capacity to diagnose the early signs of excessive drinking.

For a long time the French approach to coping with alcohol problems has been identified with psychiatry. This has not been entirely helpful, since many problem drinkers shy away from being labelled by association with the mentally ill. The 'Healthy Diet Centres' are still in their early stages. Even so, they do promise a means of achieving an earlier identification of alcohol problems. It is hoped that they will be developed and extended.

12 POLICIES IN AUSTRALIA

Denis J. Travers

Australia has approximately 14 million people, most of whom live in the capital cities. The state of Victoria has almost four million people, over half living in Melbourne. Australia has the distinction of heading the English-speaking countries in alcohol consumption, principally in the form of beer — around 1,900 million litres annually — but increasingly in the form of wines. In 1976 *per capita* alcohol consumption of people aged 15 and over in Australia was 13.3 litres. The corresponding levels for the United Kingdom and the USA were 9.1 and 10.7. It is estimated that around five per cent of adult males and one per cent of adult females are definably alcoholic, totalling approximately 300,000 people in Australia (Rankin, 1970).

Background

Major initiatives in respect of developing alcoholism programs for industry began in Australia in 1972 when the nationally-important Annual School of Studies on Alcohol and Drugs held at St Vincent's Hospital, Melbourne, was devoted to the role of industry and commerce in relation to alcohol and drug dependence (Santamaria, 1972). What emerged was a general awakening amongst doctors, social workers, personnel involved in the treatment of alcoholism, management and union leaders, that the workplace was a most suitable arena within which the fight against alcoholism can occur. At that time, there was one company in the whole of Australia with a formal policy about employees with drinking problems. That company was Kodak Australasia Pty. Ltd. Within six years, the number of alcoholism-in-industry programs was to grow to 127, 74 in private industry and 53 in the public or civil service. Seventy-eight of the 127 programs were in the state of Victoria, covering some ten per cent of that state's workforce.

During 1972/3, leaders of Victoria's management and union organisations met together with representatives of the Victorian Foundation on Alcoholism and Drug Dependence to plan activities aimed at stimulating business interest in the subject of alcoholism in the workplace.

The chief activist was Victoria's leading union spokesman, the Secretary of the Victorian Trades Hall Council, Mr K.C. Stone. He was most anxious to ensure the growth of alcoholism programs in Australia, and he had strong support from the unions he represented. Mr Stone's representation was matched on the employers' side by senior representation from employer representative organisations such as the Victorian Employers Federation, the Victorian Chamber of Manufacturers, the Victorian Chamber of Commerce, and the Victorian Public Service Board. These representatives formed a committee to plan Victoria's first conference for industry on the subject. That conference was held on 7 August 1973 in Melbourne, and was aimed at the policy-makers of managements and unions. Of the 121 delegates who attended, 33 per cent represented senior management and 16 per cent middle management, giving a total management representation of 49 per cent; 27 per cent represented unions and the remaining 24 per cent were in the health, welfare and allied professions. At the conclusion of the proceedings, the conference delegates expressed their concern about the effects of alcoholism on health and productivity and produced a number of recommendations, one of which called for the continuation of the committee's activities. The committee had as its chairman, Sir Edward Dunlop, President of the Victorian Foundation on Alcoholism and Drug Dependence (VFADD). The committee sought to meet under the Founation's banner because the members regarded the Foundation as being the most appropriate body with which to be identified and as having the necessary flexibility in its program operations and deliberations; furthermore, activities could occur within the context of the Foundation's organisation without the creation of yet another organisation in the alcohol and drug dependence area.

Early Developments

The 1973 conference was soon followed by a regional conference in Victoria in 1974 and a second Melbourne industry conference on 30 July 1974. This conference attracted a total of 227 delegates, 40 per cent of whom represented middle and senior management, 28 per cent unions and 32 per cent members of the health, welfare and allied professions. The conference resolved that the community should continue to explore preventive education aspects relative to industrial alcoholism and to draw up recommendations.

One of the members of the committee was Dr J.R. Moon, a vice-president of VFADD, but at that time also President of the national body, the Australian Foundation on Alcoholism and Drug Dependence (AFADD). During 1973/4, AFADD received a substantial grant from the Australian Government which then enabled it to appoint its first full-time executive director and establish a permanent secretariate in Canberra, the nation's capital. Until this time, AFADD played a strong encouraging and supporting role to the states and their activities in the industrial area, with considerable backing given to Victoria. At the same time the alcoholism-in-industry movement started to gain strength within its own framework and professional area. Mr Stone, in addition to being the Secretary of the Victorian Trades Hall Council, was an executive member of the Australian Council of Trade Unions, the most prominent organisation of unions in Australia. In much the same way as a state committee was established in Victoria, so too was a national committee established for Australia — the National Alcohol and Drug Dependence Industry Committee (NADDIC). Its representatives on the employers' side represented the Australian Council of Employer Federations and the Australian Chambers of Manufacturers Association. As occurred at the state level, the national body formed itself under the allegiance of the Australian Foundation.

Recent Developments

In 1975, there was a formalisation of association between NADDIC and the committees in the various states. In February 1977, the Australian Government granted AFADD sufficient funds to employ industry program co-ordinators in each state, some 18 months after funding the first such industry liaison officer in Victoria, attached to the Victorian Foundation (VFADD). This grant came about largely as a result of representations made by senior representatives from NADDIC and AFADD to the Prime Minister, the Hon Malcolm Fraser. The sum involved in the grant was A$100,000 which was particularly significant at that time because the treasury was cutting back on payments to health and welfare programs and directives had been issued to the effect that no new programs would receive funding. That the Prime Minister himself directed that this allocation should be made was a sign of the importance placed on industry programs by his government and the Australian community. This importance is seen in the direct pressure being brought to bear on the Prime Minister not only by the members of NADDIC, but also by the key management and union people in Australia including Mr G. Polites of the Associated Chambers of Manufacturers, and Mr R.J.Hawke, President of the Australian Council of Trade Unions. It is quite apparent that much of the success of the development of alcoholism-in-industry programs in Australia is due to the leadership and initial thrust provided at the highest levels of management, unions and government, especially during a time of industrial and economic discomfort.

Leadership

A key feature of alcoholism-in-industry programs as they have developed in Australia is that they are not health and welfare programs as such. They are promoted on the basis of an industry approach in line with standard techniques of detection and intervention. The appeal that alcoholism programs have for industrial leaders is that the application of suitable management supervisory techniques provides the greatest source of help for people in need.

The industry program concept is catching on in Australia because it has the support of management and unions at the highest levels. Without top-level support, alcoholism programs cannot get off the ground. If the Victorian Trades Hall Council, through its secretary, Mr Stone, had not given its support in the early days of program development, Australia would most likely still be in the dim dark days of having but one program.

Supervision

In alcoholism programs new problems are not manufactured, but rather existing ones are simply uncovered: 'The real contribution of alcoholism, through work absence, accidents, inefficiency, and staff turnover, is recognised and these problems are then diminished' (Drew, Moon and Buchanan, 1974). The notable feature of programs in Australia is that the personnel employed by the Foundations and responsible for selling the concept and servicing the programs are generally not health or welfare professionals as such, nor are they necessarily recovered alcoholics who are members of Alcoholics Anonymous. Rather they have a specific background in industry. They understand industrial matters, principles of management and management/union relationship issues, and they use that knowledge in assisting companies to implement such programs. This background helps to reinforce the emphasis on supervision and work performance. Furthermore, excursions into irrelevancies tend to be avoided or minimised, so that academic discussions on whether alcoholism is a medical disease or not are left to those with the time and energy to engage in armchair, philosophical musings.

Personnel in industry and commerce are taught that through documentation of work performance in the areas of absenteeism, safety, quality and quantity of work, a supervisor has tangible evidence to present to the employee that he has a problem — a work-performance problem. This provides the supervisor with the lever with which he can intervene. Using the work-performance criteria, the supervisor does not have to diagnose a drinking problem: he can even stop counting the employee's drinks. The real issue as far as the supervisor is concerned is work performance.

The detection and treatment of the problem drinker is not without its difficulties, but these can be overcome if careful approaches are made. Perhaps one of the greatest difficulties confronting supervisors and people in authority is not the real or imagined opposition of the unions to a program against problem drinking, but rather an inability to assess objectively work performance. At one time, 90 per cent of the workforce earned their living by using their hands. Assessment of work performance then was an easy task. Now that manual workers represent approximately 25 per cent of the workforce and 'knowledge' workers the rest, appraisal becomes far more difficult. Management has the task of recognising the need to shift the focus for assessment away from quantitative criteria to the qualitative. The focus must change from production to people. The quality and state of being of the person who is the knowledge worker and who now comprises the majority within the public sector, determines the degree of his or her knowledge production. Those in supervisory positions need to be human barometers. They need to know when there is outside interference affecting the quality of work output. The key issue is, however, the assessment of the individual through his work performance, not through his drinking. A witch-hunt for alcoholics is counterproductive and only serves to create unnecessary resentment and to destroy the program.

In Victoria, quite a team of people has been built up to promote and service industry programs, this team currently operating under the banner of VFADD. The team consists of two industry program consultants, whose prime tasks are to promote programs and achieve necessary initial steps towards the establishment of policies, an industry training officer, a half-time project officer whose prime task is to monitor and evaluate program effectiveness, a social worker providing diagnostic consultative services and two secretaries. This team works within the total organisation of VFADD and draws on other VFADD services as required, e.g. education programs, materials and resources.

This team is a far cry from the early days of 1972 and 1973 when management and union leaders were promoting what was then seen to be just a good idea. The idea has come to fruition and many changes have occurred since the initial enthusiasms allowed for professional input and the development of experience.

The VFADD team, on the basis of practical experience, has found it necessary to move away from the well-accepted American approach and to lay down some strict guidelines suitable for and applicable to Australian industry. Consequently some eight stages have been laid down as being essential for the establishment of an effective alcoholism program in a company, and these will now be discussed.

Operations in Practice

1. Initial Discussions. Initial discussions need to be held between senior management and union leaders to explain the concept of occupational alcoholism programs and obtain agreement and commitment to the introduction of the program in the organisation. The relationship between the company and the consulting body needs to be defined and an overall program plan drawn up with specific tasks being allocated and a target date set by which the introduction of the program will be completed.

2. Policy. It is necessary to achieve union/management agreement to a carefully prepared policy, establishing the rights of the individual and the organisation in formalising an organisational commitment to the program. The policy must be promulgated so that all employees are aware of it and new employees informed about it during their induction period. Promulgation of the policy should take place on completion of supervisor training and in conjunction with awareness sessions for all employees. An example of such a policy can be seen in the Appendix.

3. Management Commitment to Policy and Program. It is essential that management must regularly demonstrate its commitment to the implementation of a policy and program. All employees must be aware that management will implement the program as promised. To achieve this, management can make regular statements of their support in company journals, on notice boards and at meetings.

4. Co-ordination. The appointment of a program co-ordinator or committee responsible for overall planning and program functioning is important. The committee should be composed of union, management and health or welfare personnel who have a keen interest in the program, or one such person should be appointed as the program co-ordinator. The role of the co-ordinator or co-ordinating committee must be clearly defined. It should include designing an administrative system by which assistance is offered to the employee with a work-performance problem. There needs to be a written statement on the program operation and procedures; written clarification of work performance identification factors; a detailed statement of the role of supervisor, diagnostician/counsellor and treatment agency in offering assistance to the troubled employee. Training should be provided as soon as possible for members of the co-ordinating committee and other key personnel.

5. Diagnostic Counselling Service. There must be an appointment of a diagnostic counselling service for problem employees. A staff member of professional standing, i.e. the occupational medical officer, social worker, welfare officer or nurse, could be appointed to this position, or a decision made to use an appropriate community service, e.g. general practitioner or community health centre, where specialist alcoholism diagnostic personnel may exist. The diagnostic counsellor will be responsible for assessing the employee's problems, and referring the employee to appropriate specialist community treatment services. The diagnostician will need to be thoroughly familiar with the signs and symptoms of alcoholism and to have established referral links with appropriate treatment services. Where in-company diagnostic counsellors are established, however, there should always be an alternative, impartial counsellor available from outside the company, and employees should be aware of this.

6. Training. Comprehensive training must be provided at two levels: (a) in-depth training for program co-ordinators, diagnosticians/

counsellors, occupational health and welfare staff, and key union personnel; and (b) supervisors and union representatives. It is necessary to plan the content of training programs in both these areas. Factors such as length of course, speakers, films and hand-out material will need to be determined. In addition to this, regular follow-up training sessions are also desirable.

7. Employee Education. General-awareness education sessions are required to: (a) inform employees of the organisation's management/ union policy regarding those suffering work performance problems; and (b) to provide an appreciation of the nature of alcoholism and to promote a responsible attitude towards alcohol use and abuse.

8. Evaluation. In the initial stages of planning the program implement-ation, a procedure needs to be established for the collection of data that will enable program evaluation. In particular, case histories need to be kept in personnel variables such as absenteeism, accident rates, workers compensation rates, etc. It is also necessary to determine who will be responsible for program evaluation and a set target for regular program assessment.

Rates of Penetration

As at 30 June 1978, the 127 programs in Australia covering a workforce of 306,500 detected 942 employees with alcohol problems. If the penetration rate is defined as the number of employees detected within the size of that workforce covered by programs, then the national penetration rate is 0.3 per cent. The Victorian picture with 78 programs covering 170,500 employees with 710 detected is 0.4 per cent.

Penetration rates need to be understood in the light that alcoholism-in-industry programs will never be 100 per cent successful, i.e. not all who are detected as having alcohol-related problems will recover. In one chemical plant in Victoria, the personnel manager was asked to outline briefly the alcoholism program that his company had. He started by saying that in his opinion, the company's program had failed, and maintained that if the supervisors in the plant had been following their roles properly, a larger proportion of the estimated problem-employees should have been confronted. He indicated that in the first few months of the program, four employees had been confronted and of those, only one was still in employment at that plant. Of the remaining three, two had left the plant and returned to their previous employers and were known to be still progressing satisfactorily. The fourth person rejected help and was dismissed from the plant.

The employee who remained in employment in the plant went through a treatment program, returned to the company to work satisfactorily, and has since received a substantial promotion. The personnel manager was advised that with a success rate of 75 per cent and a penetration rate of 0.66 per cent (four detected out of 600 employees) his company's program compared favourably with elsewhere and should not be regarded as a failure.

Conclusions

There is substantial recognition by Australian industry of the human suffering and losses brought about by alcohol-related problems. Refined and well-developed alcoholism programs are becoming a part of the industrial and commercial scene, due in the main to the initial impetus provided at the highest level of management and union organisations and government. Hand in hand with the development of occupational alcoholism programs is an increasing awareness and understanding of the nature of alcohol dependence across the strata of Australian society. This is reflected particularly in the medical, social work and nursing professions to the point where there is emerging a desire and willingness to intervene in the progression of alcohol dependence at the earliest stages possible so that afflicted people can be offered a range of helping services at times when their social and employment situations may assist rather than prejudice successful recovery. The treatment of alcoholism is undergoing something of the nature of a revolution in Australia because of the attempts to provide offers to of help as soon as possible Industry is accepting the challenge as are other groups in the community, with the result that programs of tangible benefit are being produced. The days of broad, sweeping and vague aims and objectives are past and the community as a whole is starting to accept more of its own responsibilities in the alcoholism area. Industry is a significant part of that movement.

Appendix: Policy on Alcoholism and Other Dependencies

(A suggested policy which needs to be adapted to the individual company concerned.)

(1) Alcoholism is recognised as a highly complex condition which is treatable. For the purpose of this policy, alcoholism or problem drinking is defined as a condition in which an individual's consumption of any alcoholic beverage definitely and repeatedly interferes with his or her job performance and health.

(2) Problem drinking becomes a concern of (company/organisation) when it interferes with an individual's job performance. To drink or not to drink socially is the prerogative of an individual; the social stigma often associated with alcoholism has no basis in fact. A realistic recognition of this illness will encourage personnel to take advantage of available treatment.

(3) Early identification of the condition increases the treatment possibilities, and a co-operative approach by (company) and by representatives of associations and unions will encourage the afflicted to obtain treatment without delay.

(4) The decision to undertake treatment is the responsibility of the individual. It leave of absence is required, normal sickness benefits will apply. In the event that the person concerned has no sick-leave credits, social service benefits can be applied for. *Job security in these cirumstances is ensured.*

(5) When a person chooses to seek treatment and supportive assistance (company) will view him or her favourably. Job security or promotional opportunities will not be jeopardised by a decision to seek treatment.

(6) Where a person refuses the assistance offered under this policy, he or she must accept responsibility for the standard of their work and behaviour on the job, and are subject to normal discipline.

(7) This policy covers *all* personnel employed by (company) and is a joint policy statement of the relevant associations, unions and management,

or

This policy covers *all* personnel employed by (company). It has been discussed with and agreed to by the relevant staff associations and trade unions.

(8) Anyone who feels that he or she is developing, or already has a problem with drinking or other dependencies, can discuss the matter with those who are able to refer a person to the appropriate agency.

Confidentiality is guaranteed.

(9) Where the appointed officer determines that an individual
may be suffering from alcoholism or other dependencies, the officer
will refer the employee to the Victorian Foundation on Alcoholism and
Drug Dependence (VFADD) Counselling and Referral Service.

(10) Under the direction of VFADD the board will undertake to
educate all managerial and supervisory staff in the implementation and
continuing operation of this policy and understanding of its implications
by all personnel. Employees who would prefer to obtain assistance
themselves may contact the counsellor at VFADD, on telephone
63 4848.

NOTHING IN THIS STATEMENT OF POLICY IS TO BE INTER-
PRETED AS CONSTITUTING ANY WAIVER OF RESPONSIBILITY
TO MAINTAIN NORMAL DISCIPLINE STANDARDS, OR THE
RIGHTS TO INVOKE DISCIPLINARY MEASURES IN THE CASE
OF MISCONDUCT WHICH MAY RESULT FROM, OR BE
ASSOCIATED WITH, THE USE OF ALCOHOL.

REFERENCES

A'Brook, M.F., Hailstone, J.D. and McLaughlan, I.E.J. (1967), Psychiatric illness in the medical profession, *British Journal of Psychiatry 113*, 1013–23

Aitken, P.P. (1978), *Ten-to-Fourteen-Year-Olds and Alcohol* (HMSO, Edinburgh)

AMA Council on Mental Health (1973), The sick physician, *Journal of the American Medical Association 223*, 684–7

Amark, C. (1970), A study of alcoholism, *Acta Psychiatrica et Neurologica Scandinavica supplementum 70*, 237–43

Andenaes, J. and Sørensen, R.K. (1979), Alkohol og dødsulykker i trafikken, *Norsk Juridisk Tidoskrift Lov og Ret 5*, 83–109

Andreski, A. (1974), *Social Science as Sorcery* (Penguin, Harmondsworth)

Anonymous (1977a), *Tartan Star* (Scottish & Newcastle Breweries Ltd., company newspaper) *78*, 4; (1977b) *79*, 6

Arbeidsdirekotoratet 7 (1979), *Kontor: Arbeidstreningstiltak for Ungdoms-Evaluering* (Stencil, Osk)

Arner, O. (1973), The role of alcohol in fatal accidents among seamen, *British Journal of Addiction 68*, 185–9

Arnoux, H. (1972), Contribution a l'etude de la lutte contre l'alcoolisme dans la region de Carpentras (MD Thesis, Marseilles)

Barrett, T.M. (1943), Chronic alcoholism in veterans, *Quarterly Journal of Studies on Alcohol 1*, 68–78

Berglin, C.G. and Rosengren, E. (1974), The capacity for work and pension-ability of 868 alcoholics (in Swedish), *Swedish Medical Journal 71*, 3520

Bissell, L. and Jones, R.W. (1976), The alcoholic physician: a survey, *American Journal of Psychiatry 133*, 1142–6

Blacky, K.D. and Rosow, I. (1973), Physicians who kill themselves, *Archives of General Psychiatry 29*, 800–5

Blacklaws, A.F. (1978), The drink problem in industry, *Brewing Review* (Jan/Feb), 10–12

Blaxter, M. (1979), *Shetland Survey of Alcohol Problems in General Practice* (Shetland Health Board and Shetland Medical Committee)

Board of Trade (1969), *Trawler Safety. Final Report of the Committee of Inquiry into Trawler Safety* (HMSO, London)

Borg, A. (1970), *Alkoholen i Sarnfunn-søkonomien Ressurser som Destrueres pga Alkoholkonsurn* (Stencil, Industrikonsulert O/S Oslo)

Bresard, M. (1971), *Incidence de malnutrition par le consommation d'alcool sur le niveau de salaire* (Le Symposium International d'Alimentation et Travail, Vittel)

Bressler, B. (1976), Suicide and drug abuse in the medical community, *Suicide and Life-Threatening Behaviour 6*, 169–78

Brewer's Statistical Handbook (1976) (Brewing Publications Ltd., London)

Brun-Gulbrandsen, S. and Irgens-Jensen, O. (1967), Abuse of alcohol amongst seamen, *British Journal of Addiction 62*, 19–27

Bruun, K., Edwards, G., Lumio, M., Makela, K., Pan, L., Popham, R.E., Room, R., Schmidt, W., Skog, O-J., Sulkenen, P. and Osterberg, E. (1975), *Alcohol Control Policies in Public Health Perspective* (Finnish Foundation for Alcohol Studies, Helsinki)

Butcher, C.H.H. (1978), Legal aspects, in *Abuse of Alcohol among Medical Practitioners* (Joint Symposium of the Medical Council on Alcoholism and the Society for the Study of Addiction, London)

Cadenhead, R.McN. (1976), Hospital admissions of fishermen from the fishing grounds around the Shetland Islands, *Journal of Social and Occupational Medicine 26*, 127–31

Cahalan, D. and Cisin, I.H. (1966), American drinking practices: Summary of findings from a national probability sample. II. Measurement of massed versus spaced drinking, *Quarterly Journal of Studies on Alcohol 29*, 130–54, 642–58

Cahalan, D. and Room, R. (1974), *Problem Drinking Aming American Men* (Publication Division, Rutgers Center of Alcohol Studies, New Brusnwick, New Jersey)

Cargill, D. (1976), Scotch and Irish, *World Medicine* (16 June), 22–4

Carney, M.W.P. (1963), Alcoholic hallucinocis among servicemen in Cyprus, *Journal of the Royal Army Medical Corps 109*, 104–70

Carney, M.W.P. and Lawes, T.G.G. (1967), The etiology of alcoholism in the English upper classes, *Quarterly Journal of Studies on Alcohol 28*, 59–69

Cartwright, A.K.J., Shaw, S.J. and Spratley, T.A. (1978), The relationships between *per capita* consumption, drinking patterns and alcohol-related problems in a population sample 1965–74. Part II: Implications for alcohol control policy, *British Journal of Addiction 73*, 254–6

Cavalie (1955), Problemes poses au medecin du travail des travaux publics par l'ethyisme chronique (Communication a la Societe de Medicine du Travail de la Region, Toulousaine, June)

Clark, R.E. (1949), The relationships of alcoholic psychosis commitment rates to occupational income and occupational prestige, *American Sociological Review 14*, 539–43

Cohen, J., Dearnley, E.J. and Hansell, C.E. (1958), The role taken in driving under the influence of alcohol, *British Medical Journal 1*, 1438

Comite National de Defense Contre L'Alcoolisme (1969 and 1970), *Alcoolisme, Maladie Sociale* (Actes du Congres de Versailles, Alcool ou Sante, nos 5 and 1)
—— (1976), *Plan Type d'un Programme d'Action Antialcoolique d'Enterprise*, 7. Also: *Legislation et Information Antialcoolique sur les Vieux de Travail*, 9. (Documentation permanente, Paris)

Cramond, W.A. (1969), Anxiety in medical practice. The doctor's own anxiety, *Australian and New Zealand Medical Journal 3*, 324–9

Davies, J.B. and Stacey, B.G. (1972), *Teenagers and Alcohol* (HMSO, London)

Davies, J.B., Cochrane, J. and Marini, C. (1977/8), *Alcohol and Work* (Report prepared for the Scottish Council on Alcoholism)

Davies, J.B. (1978), Reported alcohol consumption, and the attitudes of managerial and non-managerial employees, in a study of five industries on Clydeside, *British Journal on Alcohol and Alcoholism 13*, (*4*), 160–9

Delahaye, S. (1977), An analysis of clients using alcoholic agencies within one community service, in Madden, J.S., Walker, R. and Kenyon, W.H. (eds.), *Alcoholism and Drug Dependence: A Multidisciplinary Approach* (New York, Plenum), 335–54

Denes, A.E., Smith, J.L., Maynard, J.E., Dofo, I., Berghist, K.R. and Finkel, A.J. (1978), 'Hepatitis B' infection in physicians, *Journal of the American Medical Association 239*, 210–12

Department of Health, Education and Welfare (1978), *Alcohol and Health* (Third Report to Congress, Washington, D.C.)

Department of Health for Scotland (1935), *Report on Incapacitating Sickness in the Insured Population of Scotland during the year 1st July, 1933 to 30th June, 1934* (HMSO, Edinburgh)

Department of Trade (1975), *Report of the Working Group on Discipline in the*

Fishing Industry (HMSO, London)

De Roumanie, M. (1979), Preliminary results of WHO survey of drinking habits and alcohol-related problems (Scottish Section) (paper presented at 7th Scottish Alcohol Research Symposium, Pitlochry)

Desanti, E. and Aillaud, Y. (1971), L'ethylisme dans la region Marselllaise, *Corse-Mediterranee Medicale 198*, 2, 51–64

Dight, S. (1976), *Scottish Drinking Habits* (Office of Population Censuses and Surveys, Social Survey Division, HMSO, London)

Doll, R. and Peto, R. (1976), Mortality in relation to smoking: 20 years' observations on male British doctors, *British Medical Journal 2*, 1525–36

Drew, L.R., Moon, J.R. and Buchanan, F.H. (1974), *Alcoholism, a Handbook* (William Heinemann, Melbourne)

Druckker, W., Goodie, B., Russel, R.I. and Chaudwri, A.K.R. (1972), Evidence for a role of hepatitis B in chronic alcoholic liver disease, *Lancet 2*, 724–5

Druckker, W., Schoutten, W.A.G. and Alberts, C.H.R. (1968), Epidemic hepatitis in a renal dialysis unit, *Proceedings of the European Dialysis and Transplant Association 239*, 210–12

Duckert, F. (1978), *Attføring au Stoff – og Alkohol Misbrukers – Erfaringer fra et Proveprosjekt* (Tylkesar beidskontoret for osk og Akershus, Osk)

Duffy, J.C. and Litin, E.M. (1964), Psychiatric morbidity of physicians, *Journal of the American Medical Association 189*, 989–92

Edwards, G., Kellog-Fisher, M., Hawker, A. and Hensman, C. (1967), Clients of alcoholism information centres, *British Medical Journal 4*, 364

Edwards, G., Chandler, J. and Hensman, C. (1972), Drinking in a London suburb, I, *Quarterly Journal of Studies on Alcohol, supplement 6*, 69–93

Edwards, G. (1975), The alcoholic doctor: a case of neglect, *Lancet 2*, 1297–8

Edwards, G. and Orford, J. (1977), Alcoholism: a controlled trial of treatment and advice, *Journal of Studies on Alcohol 38,(5)*, 1004–31

Eiser, J.R., Sutton, S.R. and Wober, M. (1977), Smokers, non-smokers and the attribution of addiction, *British Journal of Social and Clinical Psychology 16*, 329–36

Faurobert, L. (1971), *Le Risque Alcool dans l'Enterprise* (Les Editions Ouvrieres, Paris)

Ferguson, D. (1973), Smoking, drinking and non-narcotic analgesic habits in an occupational group, *Medical Journal of Australia 1*, 1271

Frank, H., Heil, W. and Leodolter, I. (1967), The liver and beer consumption, *Munchener Medizinische Wochenschrift 109*, 892–97

Franklin, R.A. (1977), One hundred doctors at the Retreat, *British Journal of Psychiatry 131*, 11–14

Gautier, F. (1965), The industrial development in the control of alcoholism, the value of the ricossery test (in French), *Rev. Alcoholism 11*, 312

General Medical Council (1974), *Complaints Against Doctors* (GMC Annual Report, London)

Gervois and Dubois (1977), Correlations physio-pathologiques alcool-tabac, in *Pollutions Individuelles et Maladies de Civilisation* (Sandoz, Paris), 30–9

Glatt, M.M. and Hills, D.R. (1965), Occupational behaviour patterns in samples of English alcoholic employees, *British Journal of Addiction 61*, 71

Glatt, M.M. (1967), Complications of alcoholism in the social sphere, *British Journal of Addiction 62*, 35–44

———— (1974), Alcoholism among doctors, *Lancet 2*, 342–3

———— (1976), *Alcoholism* (Hodder and Stoughton, London)

———— (1978), Alcohol abuse among medical practitioners, in *Abuse of Alcohol among Medical Practitioners* (Joint Symposium of the Medical Council and the Society for the Study of Addiction, London)

Godard, J. (1955), La mortalite masculine et milieu industriel et ses rapports avec l'alcoolisme, *Archives des Maladies Professionalles 16*, 6

────── (1956), *La Prevention de l'Alcoolisme a l'Usine* (Ed. de l'Entreprise Modern, Paris)

────── (1964), Alcoolisme et medecine du travail, *Revue du Practicien XIV, 4*, 437–40

────── (1969), Alcoolisme et medecine du travail. Une enquete aupres des medecins du travail, *Revue de L'Alcoolisme 16, 1*, 4–24

────── (1970), Medecine du travail et alcoolisme. Une enquete aupres des medecins du travail, *Revue de l'Alcoolisme 1*, 9–24

────── (1973), *Alcoolisme, Encyclopedie de Medicine, d'Hygiene et de Securite du Travail, vol. 1* (Bureau International du Travail, Geneva)

────── (1975), *Le Medecin du Travail et l'Alcoolisme*, 2nd edn (Documentation Francaise, Paris)

Godard, J., Durrmeyer, G. and Delabroise, M. (1966). Problems humains poses par l'evolution technologique dans l'industrie siderurgique. *L'Evolution Medicale 10*, 4

Goldberg, L. (1943), Quantitative studies of alcohol tolerance in man, *Acta Physiologica Scandinavia, suppl 16*

Goodwin, D.W., Schulsinger, F., Hermansen, L., Guze, S.B. and Winokur, G. (1973), Alcohol problems in adoptees raised apart from alcoholic biological parents, *Archives of General Psychiatry 28*, 238–43

Grant, G.L. (1961), An essay on fishermen, their health and their society (dissertation for the Diploma in Public Health, Aberdeen, University of Aberdeen; cited in Moore, 1969a)

Graz, L. (1973), On the great waters, *World Health* (July–August), 28–47

Green, R.C., Carroll, G.J. and Buxton, W.D. (1976), Drug addiction among physicians, *Journal of the American Medical Association 236*, 1372–5

Gunderson, E.K.E. and Schuckit, M.A. (1975), Hospitalization rates for alcoholism in the navy and marine corps, *Diseases of the Nervous System 36*, 681–4

Gwinner, P.D.V. (1976), The treatment of alcoholics in a military context, *Journal of Alcoholism 11*, 24–31

Haas, R.M. (1970), L'Alcoolisme dans l'industrie, in *L'Alcoolisme en France* (La Documentation Francaize, Paris), 34–40

────── (1971), *Milieu du Travail et Alcoolisme* (Haut Comite d'Etude et d'Information sur l'Alcoolisme, Documentation Francaise, Paris), 78

Harrington, L.G. and Price, A.C. (1962), Alcoholism in a geriatric setting, *Journal of the American Geriatric Society 10*, 197–211

Heath, B.G. (1945), Group psychotherapy and alcohol addiction, *Quarterly Journal of Studies on Alcohol 5*, 555–62

Henderson, R.M. and Bacon, S.D. (1953), Problem drinking: the Yale plan for business and industry, *Quarterly Journal of Studies on Alcohol 14*, 247–62

Heyman, M.M. (1978), *Alcoholism Programs in Industry, monograph no. 12* (Rutgers Center for Alcohol Studies, Publications Division, New Brunswick, New Jersey)

Hore, B.D. and Smith, E. (1975), Who goes to alcoholic units? *British Journal of Addiction 70*, 263–70

Jahoda, G. and Cramond, J. (1972), *Children and Alcohol* (HMSO, London)

J.I.F. (1947), Alcoholism: an occupational disease in seamen, *Quarterly Journal of Studies on Alcohol 8*, 498–505

Jellinek, E.M. (1960), *The Disease Concept of Alcoholism* (College University Press, New Haven)

Jindra, N.J. and Forslund, M.A. (1978), Alcoholics Anonymous in a western US city, *Journal of Studies on Alcohol 39*, 110–20

Johnson, P., Armor, D.J., Polich, S. and Stambul, H. (1977), *US Adult Drinking Practices: Time Trends, Social Correlates and Sex Roles* (Final report of NIAAA Contract ADM-281-76-0020, Rand Corporation, Santa Monica, California)

Jones, R.E. (1977), A study of 100 physician psychiatric inpatients, *American Journal of Psychiatry 134*, 1119–23

Kitchen, J. (1977), *Labour Law and Off-shore Oil* (Croom Helm, London)

Kolb, D. and Gunderson, E.K.E. (1977), Alcoholism in the United States Navy, *Armed Forces and Society 3*, 183–94

Kreitman, N. (1977), Three themes in the epidemiology of alcoholism, in Edwards, G. and Grant, M. (eds.), *Alcoholism: New Knowledge and New Responses* (Croom Helm, London; University Park Press, Baltimore), 48–59

Labour-Management Alcoholism Journal (1974a), *A Joint Union-Management Approach to Alcoholism Recovery Programs*

Labour-Management Alcoholism Journal (1974b), *4 (1)*, 37, also *4 (3)*, 23–4

Lanesskog, J. (1978), Arbeidstrenings-prosjekt for personer med problemer – VALO – prosjektet, *Sosialt Forum, 9, 5*, 153–6

Le Go, Valette, Pertusier and Gillard (1963), La lutte antialcoolique dans une grande collectivitie de travail, *Revue de l'Alcoolisme 1*

Le Go, P.M. and Pertusier, J.M. (1971), Methode de depistage de la deterioration ethylique a l'aide de la grille cotee (Ed. Medicales, L.P.F., Paris), 27

Ledermann, S. (1956), *Alcool, Alcoolisme, Alcoolisation*, Institut National d'Etudes Demographiques, Travaux et Documents, Cahier no. 29 (Presses Universitaires de France, Paris)

Lehman, G. (1955), *Praktische Arbeitsphysiologie* (Georg Thieme Verlag, Stuttgart, 1953; French translation, Editions d'Organization, Paris), 44

Lemere, F., Maxwell, M.A. and O'Hollaren, P. (1956), Sociological survey of 7,828 patients treated for alcoholism, *Journal of Nervous and Mental Disorders 123*, 281–5

Lereboullet, J. (1972), *L'Alcoolisme* (Bailliere, Paris)

Long, J.R., Hewitt, L.E. and Blane, H.T. (1956), Alcohol use in the armed forces: a review. II: Problem areas and recommendations, *Military Medicine 142*, 120–8

Ludlam, J.E. (1976), Physician rehabilitation: a better alternative to punishment, *Hospital Medical Staff 5*, 8–11

Mair, A. (1979), A study of occupational health services in the trawler industry (personal communication)

Mair, A. and Deans, J.P. (1979), Injuries and illnesses of fishermen treated at Scrabster, Caithness (personal communication)

Maletsky, B.M. and Klotter, J. (1975), The prevalence of alcoholism in a military hospital, *Military Medicine 140*, 273–5

Matilla, M. (ed.) (1976), *Alcohol, Drugs and Driving. Modern Problems of Pharmaco-Psychiatry, vol. II* (S. Karger, Basel)

Mayer, J. and Myerson, D.J. (1970), Characteristics of outpatient alcoholics in relation to change in drinking, work and marital status during treatment, *Quarterly Journal of Studies on Alcohol 31*, 889–97

Merseyside Council on Alcoholism (1973), *The Alcohol Explosion* (Tenth Annual Report, Liverpool)

Metz, B. and Marcoux, F. (1960), Alcoolisation et accidents du travail, *Revue de L'Alcoolisme 6*, 3

Metz, B. (1964), Les boissons en milieu industrial, *Bulletin de la Societe Scientifique Alimentaire 52*, 4

Milstead-O'Keefe, R.T. and Brooks-McLaine, P. (1979). Outpatient programmes for workers and their families, in *Proc. 25th Int. Inst. for the Prevention and Treatment of Alcoholism* (ICAA Case Postale 140, Lausanne 1001, Switzerland)

Modlin, H.C. and Montes, A. (1964), Narcotics addiction in physicians, *American Journal of Psychiatry 121*, 358–63

Moore, S.R.W. (1969a), The occupation of trawl fishing and the medical aid available to the Grimsby deep sea fishermen, *British Journal of Industrial Medicine 26*, 1–24

—— (1969b), The mortality and morbidity of deep sea fishermen sailing from Grimsby in one year, *British Journal of Industrial Medicine 26*, 25–46

Morice, P.A. (1954), La responsabilite de l'alcoolisme dans les accidents du travail, *Revue de l'Alcoolisme 3*, 129–33

Murray, R.M. (1975), Alcoholism and employment, *Journal of Alcoholism 10*, 23–6

—— (1976a), Alcoholism amongst male doctors in Scotland, *Lancet* (October 2), 729–31

—— (1976b), Characteristics and prognosis of alcoholic doctors, *British Medical Journal 2*, 1537–9

—— (1977), Psychiatric illness in male doctors and controls: an analysis of Scottish hospitals' 'in-patient data', *British Journal of Psychiatry 131*, 1–10

National Council on Alcoholism (1976), *A Joint Union-Management Approach to Alcoholism Recovery Programs* (NCA, London), 5

—— (1977), *Report of the Working Party on Alcohol and Work, 1977* (obtainable from NCA, 3 Grosvenor Street, London, SW1), 74

National Transportation Safety Board, Railroad Accident Report (1974), *Rear End Collision of Two Southern Pacific Transportation Company Freight Trains* (Report no. NTSB-RAR-74-1, Washington, D.C.)

Niveau (1977), L'action antialcoolique aux Houilleres du Bassin de Lorraine, *Cahiers du Comite National de Defense Contre L'Alcoolisme* (Paris), 31

Noie, N. (1977), Medicine's response to the disabled doctor problem: Help our colleagues, protect their patients, *Hospital Medical Staff 6*, 9–14

Norris, J.L. (1972), Point de vue syndical sur l'alcoolisme et la toxicomanie, *Revue International du Travail 106*, 4

Nyden, P.J. (1978), Alcohol consumption among appalachian coal miners: speculations and proposals for further investigations (paper presented at Intramural Research Workshop of Occupational Conditions and Alcohol Consumption, Elkridge, Maryland, USA)

Observer and Maxwell, M.A. (1959). Study of absenteeism, accidents and sickness payments in problem drinkers in industry, *Quarterly Journal of Studies on Alcoholism 20*, 302

Ødegaard, O. (1956), The incidence of psychoses in various occupations, *International Journal of Social Psychiatry 2*, 85–104

Office of Population Censuses and Surveys (1978), *Decennial Supplement England and Wales 1970–72 on Occupational Mortality* (HMSO, London). Also earlier supplements relating to 1911, 1921, 1931, 1951 and 1961

Orford, J. and Edwards, G. (1977), *Alcoholism* (Oxford University Press, Oxford)

Pell, S. and D'Alonzo, C.A. (1970), Sickness, absenteeism and alcoholics, *Journal of Occupational Medicine 12*, 198

Pequinot, G. (1955). Enquete citee dans: Brunard, J. *Rapport sur le Cout Annuel et la Prevention de l'Alcoolisme* (Presidence du Conseil), 92

Perlis, L. (1977), Unionism and alcoholism, in Schramm, C.J. (ed.), *Alcoholism and its Treatment in Industry* (Johns Hopkins University Press, Baltimore)

Perrin, P. (1960 and 1961), L'alcoolisme, *Syntheses Cliniques Jean Garnier 89*, 91, 93

Pettigrew, N.M., Goudie, R.B., Russell, R.I. and Chaudhwri, A.K.R. (1972), Evidence for the role of hepatitis B in chronic alcoholic liver disease, *Lancet 2*, 724–5

Plant, M.A., Kreitman, N., Miller, T. and Duffy, J. (1977), Observing public drinking, *Journal of Studies on Alcohol 38 (5)*, 867–80

Plant, M.A. (1978), Occupation and alcoholism: cause or effect? A controlled study of recruits to the drink trade, *International Journal of the Addictions 13 (4)*, 605–26

———— (1979a), *Drinking Careers, Occupations, Drinking Habits and Drinking Problems* (Tavistock, London)

———— (1979b), Estimating drinking patterns and the prevalence of alcohol-related problems, *British Journal on Alcohol and Alcoholism 14 (3)*, 132–9

Plant, M.A. and Pirie, F. (1979), Self-reported alcohol consumption and alcohol-related problems: a study in four Scottish towns, *Social Psychiatry 14*, 65–73

Plant, M.L. and Plant, M.A. (1979), Self-reported alcohol consumption and other characteristics of one hundred patients attending a Scottish alcoholism treatment unit, *British Journal on Alcohol and Alcoholism 14 (4)*, 197–207

Pond, D.A. (1969), Doctors' mental health, *New Zealand Medical Journal 69*, 131–5

Powdermaker, F. (1945), Review of cases at merchant marine rest centres, *American Journal of Psychiatry 10*, 650–4

Quenu (1955), Cite dans: Brunard, J. *Rapport sur le Cout Annuel et la Prevention de l'Alcoolisme* (Presidence du Conseil), 92

Rankin, J.E. (1970), *Size and Nature of the Misuse of Alcohol and Drugs in Australia* (Proceedings of 29th International Congress on Alcoholism and Drug Dependence, Sydney)

Report to the EEC (1979), *The Medico-Social Risks of Alcohol Consumption* (EEC, Luxembourg)

Reynolds, J., Mannello, T.A. and Seaman, F.J. (1978), *Estimating Prevalance and Cost of Alcohol Abuse on Railroads and Evaluating Railroad Employee Assistance Programs* (University Research Corporation, Washington, D.C.)

Richardson, W.T. (1979), Alcohol and deep sea fisherman (personal communication)

Ritson, E.B. (1968), The prognosis of alcohol addicts treated by a specialised unit, *British Journal of Psychiatry 114*, 1019

Ritson, E.B. and Hassall, C. (1970), *The Management of Alcoholism* (E. and S. Livingstone, Edinburgh)

Rix, K.J.B., Hunter, D. and Olley, P.C. (1977), Alcoholism and the fishing industry in NE Scotland (paper presented at 3rd Scottish Alcohol Research Symposium, Loch Achray)

———— (in preparation), The incidence of alcoholism in north-east Scotland fishermen, 1966–70

Rix, K.J.B. (1978), Drinking, gambling and wenching: another review of Bozzy (personal communication)

Robinson, D. (1972), The alcohologist's addiction: some implications of having lost control over the disease concept of alcoholism, *Quarterly Journal of Studies on Alcohol 33 (4)*, 1028–42

———— (1979), *Talking Out of Alcoholism: The Self-Help Process of Alcoholics Anonymous* (Croom Helm, London; University Park Press, Baltimore)

Roman, R.M. and Trice, H.M. (1970). The development of deviant drinking behaviour. Occupation risk factors, *Archives of Environmental Health 20*, 424–35

—— (1972), Deviance and work: the influence of alcohol and drugs on work behaviours, *Reviews on Enviornmental Health 1*, 9–51

Rose, H.K. and Glatt, M.M. (1961), A study of alcoholism as an occupational hazard of merchant seamen, *Journal of Mental Science 107*, 18–30

Rose, K.D. and Rosow, I. (1973), Physicians who kill themselves, *Archives of General Psychiatry 29*, 800–5

Royal College of Psychiatrists (1979), *Alcohol and Alcoholism* (Tavistock, London), 79–80

Saad, E.S.N. and Madden, J.S. (1976), Certified incapacity and unemployment in alcoholics, *British Journal of Psychiatry 128*, 340

Santamaria, Joseph N. (ed.) (1972), *Summer School of Studies on Alcohol and Drugs* (St Vincent's Hospital, Melbourne)

Sauvy, A. (1971), Un Mal anachronique, *La Sante de l'Homme* (January-February), 4–8

Schilling, R.S.F. (1966), Trawler fishing. An extreme occupation, *Proceedings of the Royal Society of Medicine 59*, 405–10

Schilling, R.S.F., Walford, J. and Wood, R. (1969), The mortality of fishermen in Great Britain, Appendix B, in Board of Trade (1969)

Schramm, C.J. (ed.) (1977), *Alcoholism and its Treatment in Indutry* (Johns Hopkins University Press, Baltimore)

Schramm, C.J., Mandell, W. and Archer, J. (1978), *Workers Who Drink* (Lexington Books, Lexington, Mass)

Schukit, M.A. and Gunderson, E.K.E. (1974), The association between alcoholism and job type in the US Navy, *Quarterly Journal of Studies on Alcohol 35*, 577–85

—— (1974a), Alcoholism among navy and marine corps officers, *Military Medicine 139*, 809–11

—— (1974b), The association between alcoholism and job type in the US Navy, *Quarterly Journal of Studies on Alcohol 35*, 577–85

Sclare, A.B. (1978a), Discussion, in *Abuse of Alcohol among Medical Practitioners* (Joint Symposium of the Medical Council on Alcoholism and the Society for the Study of Addiction, London)

—— (1978b), *Alcohol Abuse in the Armed Services* (paper presented at 2nd International Conference on Psychological Stress and Adjustment in Time of War and Peace, Jerusalem, Israel)

Scott, G. and Pottle, F.A. (eds.) (1932), *The Private Papers of James Boswell* (privately printed)

Scottish Council on Alcoholism (1975), *Alcoholism and Alcohol Abuse – a Scottish Problem* (1st Annual Report – 1974/5, Edinburgh)

Sellers, T.H. (1978), Welcoming address, in *Abuse of Alcohol among Medical Practitioners* (Joint Symposium of the Medical Council on Alcoholism and the Society for the Study of Addiction, London)

Simon, W. and Lumly, G.K. (1968), Suicide among physician-patients, *Journal of Nervous and Mental Diseases 147*, 105–12

Sissel, E. (1974), *Foreløpig rapport fra Arbeidstrening sopplegg for Ungdom.* (Stencil, Fylkesarbeidskontoret for Osk og Akershus, Osk)

Small, I.F., Small, J.C., Assne, C.M. and Moore, D.F. (1969), The fate of the mentally-ill physician, *American Journal of Psychiatry 125*, 39–48

Spratley, T.A. (1969), Occupation as a cause of alcoholism (MPhil dissertation, University of London)

Statens Edruskapdirektorat (1978), *Alkohol i Norge* (Oslo)

Stevenson, R.W. (1942), Absenteeism in an industrial plant due to alcoholism, *Quarterly Journal of Studies on Alcohol 2*, 661

Straus, R. and Winterbottom, M.T. (1949), Drinking patterns of an occupational group: domestic servants, *Quarterly Journal of Studies on Alcohol 10*, 441–60

Strega, M. (1978), Protecting the Public, *World Medicine* (22 March), 47–8

Stuart, B.S., Taylor, W.D., Templeton, A.A. and Wang, S.W.S. (1967), The fishing industry in Aberdeen and extent and nature of alcoholism among fishermen (medical students project report, University of Aberdeen, Department of Public Health and Social Medicine, unpublished)

Sundby, P. (1956), Occupation and insanity. The frequency distribution of psychosis within different occupational groups with special reference to psychosis among ordinary seamen, *Acta Psychiatrica et Neurologica Scandinavica, supplementum 106*, 276–87

Symposium (1978), *Abuse of Alcohol among Medical Practitioners* (Joint Symposium of the Medical Council on Alcoholism and the Society for the Study of Addiction, London)

Talbott, G.D., Shoemaker, K.E., Follo, M.L. and Bullard, A.L. (1976), Some dynamics of addiction among physicians, *Journal of the Medical Association of Georgia 65*, 77–83

Toone, B., Murray, R.M., Clare, A. and Creed, F. (1980), in preparation

Tor, R. (1977), Alkohol og narkstika som arbeidsplassens problem, *Tidsskrift om edruskapsspørs-mal 3*, 5, 3–4

Travers, Denis J. (1978), Prevention and education: a gloomy past, a bright future (32nd International Congress on Alcoholism and Drug Dependence, Poland)

Trice, H.M. (1965), Alcoholic employees: a comparison of psychotic neurotic and 'normal' personnel, *Journal of Occupational Medicine 7*, 94–9

Trice, H.M. and Roman, R.M. (1972), *Spirits and Demons at Work: Alcohol and Other Drugs on the Job* (New York State School of Industrial and Labor Relations, Cornell University, Ithaca, New York)

Trice, H.M. and Beyer, J.M. (1977), Differential use of an alcoholism policy in federal organisation by skill level of employees, in Schramm, C.J. (ed.), *Alcoholism and its Treatment in Industry* (Johns Hopkins University Press, Baltimore)

Tunstall, J. (1962), *The Fishermen* (MacGibbon and Kee, London)

Vaillant, G.E., Brighton, J.R. and McArthur, C. (1970), Physicians' use of mood-altering drugs, *New England Journal of Medicine 282*, 365–70

Vaillant, G.E., Sobowale, N.C. and McArthur, C. (1972), Some psychological vulnerabilities of physicians, *New England Journal of Medicine 3*, 324–9

Vincent, M.O., Robinson, E.A. and Latt, L. (1969), Physicians as patients, *Canadian Medical Association Journal 100*, 403–12

Von Wiegand, R. (1972), Alcoholism in Industry, *British Journal of Addiction 67*, 181

Wallinga, J.V. (1956), Severe alcoholism in career military personnel, *United States Armed Forces Medical Journal 7*, 551–61

Walsh, D. (1969), Alcoholism in the Republic of Ireland, *British Journal of Psychiatry 115*, 1021–5

Walton, H.J., Ritson, E.B. and Kennedy, R.I. (1966), Response of alcoholics to clinic treatment, *British Medical Journal* (12 November), 1171–4

Waring, E.M. (1974), Emotional illness in psychiatric trainees, *British Journal of Psychiatry 125*, 10–11

—— (1975), Beginning psychiatric training syndrome, *Canadian Psychiatric Association Journal 20*, 533–6

—— (1977), Medical professionals with emotional illness, *Psychiatric Journal of the University of Ottawa 2*, 161–5

Williams, S.E.V., Munford, R.S., Colton, T., Murphy, D.A. and Poskanzer, D.C.

(1971), Mortality among physicians: a short study, *Journal of Chronic Diseases 24*, 393–401

Williams, R.L. and Tramontana, J. (1977), The evaluation of occupational alcoholism programmes, in Schramm, C.J. (ed.), *Alcoholism and its Treatment in Industry* (Johns Hopkins University Press, Baltimore)

Wilkins, R.H. (1974), *The Hidden Alcoholic in General Practice* (Elek, London)

Wilson, G.B. (1940), *Alcohol and the Nation* (Nicholson and Watson, London)

NOTES ON CONTRIBUTORS

Allan F. Blacklaws: Group Personnel Director, Scottish and Newcastle Breweries Ltd, Edinburgh

John B. Davies: Lecturer, Department of Psychology, University of Strathclyde

Fanny Duckert: Psychologist, Incognito Clinic, Oslo, Norway

William S. Dunkin: Acting Director, Department of Labor-Management Services, National Council on Alcoholism Inc., New York, USA

Jacques Godard: Vice President, Comité National de Defense Contre l'Alcoolisme, Paris, and former Medical Inspector of Factories, France

Brian D. Hore: Consultant Psychiatrist, Withington Hospital, Manchester

Robin M. Murray: Senior Lecturer, Institute of Psychiatry, London

Martin A. Plant: Sociologist, Alcohol Research Group, Department of Psychiatry, University of Edinburgh

Keith J.B. Rix: Lecturer, Department of Psychiatry, University of Manchester

F. James Seaman: Social Psychologist, Independent Consultant, Arlington, Virginia, USA

Denis J. Travers: Executive Director, Victorian Foundation on Alcoholi Alcoholism and Drug Dependence, Melbourne, Australia

INDEX